The Catholic
Theological Union
LIBRARY
Chicago, Ill.

FEB 4 1976

THE PROPHETS
AND THE LAW

IN MEMORIAM

On the twenty-ninth of January 1975, just days before the appearance of this book, Richard Victor Bergren died.

His family and friends, teachers, colleagues and students, and the world of Bible scholarship have lost a great light.

ZICHRONO LIV'RACHA. The memory of this young and much loved man is an enduring blessing.

WITHDRAWN

THE PROPHETS
AND THE LAW

by

Richard Victor Bergren

The Catholic
Theological Union
LIBRARY
Chicago, Ill.

HEBREW UNION COLLEGE—JEWISH INSTITUTE OF RELIGION
CINCINNATI, NEW YORK, LOS ANGELES, JERUSALEM
1974

WITHDRAWN

© COPYRIGHT 1974 BY THE HEBREW UNION COLLEGE PRESS
HEBREW UNION COLLEGE—JEWISH INSTITUTE OF RELIGION

Library of Congress Cataloging in Publication Data

Bergren, Richard Victor.
   The prophets and the law.

   (Monographs of the Hebrew Union College, no. 4)
   Originally presented as the author's thesis,
Hebrew Union College-Jewish Institute of Religion.
   Bibliography: p.
   1. Bible. O. T. Prophets--Theology. 2. Law
(Theology)--Biblical teaching. I. Title.
II. Series: Hebrew Union College-Jewish Institute
of Religion. Monographs, no. 4.
BS1198.B45 1974   296.3   74-13370
ISBN 0-87820-403-2

MANUFACTURED IN THE UNITED STATES OF AMERICA

Published on the
GEORGE ZEPIN
Memorial Publication Fund

TABLE OF CONTENTS

FOREWORD

The Prophets and the Law is the fourth in the series of MONO-GRAPHS OF THE HEBREW UNION COLLEGE, published on occasion by the Hebrew Union College—Jewish Institute of Religion. The occasion is an important doctoral dissertation. It is published here as it was presented in 1972.

A graduate of Amherst and the Colgate Rochester Divinity School, the author Richard V. Bergren had taught for several years at Alfred University, Alfred, New York, before he entered our doctoral program in Cincinnati. He spent four years with us, at first with a grant from Alfred University and the Fund for the Advancement of Education, and then as occupant of Hebrew Union College Interfaith Fellowships. With his Doctor of Philosophy degree he returned to Alfred in 1972 to become Assistant Professor there in the Division of Human Studies.

In our opinion *The Prophets and the Law* supports the contention that an essay need not be dull to be scholarly. And it deals with prophetic priorities.

SHELDON H. BLANK,

Nelson Glueck Professor of Bible

ACKNOWLEDGEMENTS

My father is a persistent man. It seems as though it must have been at my seminary graduation that he first said, "When are you going to get your Ph.D.?" During the intervening years, he has continued to find occasion to return to the matter. It was his idea, and he persisted until it became mine. And, he has had allies.

Professors Jim Alvin Sanders at Colgate Rochester Divinity School (now of Union Theological Seminary) and George W. Anderson at the University of Durham (now at Edinburgh) early instilled in me the love of scholarship. Their scholarship I have admired; their friendship I have treasured.

President Leland Miles, Acting Dean David Leach, and Professor Myron Sibley made the first breach in the financial barrier by arranging for me to receive a generous stipend for two years from the Pre-Doctoral Support Program of Alfred University. Hebrew Union College supplemented this, first with a tuition grant, then with fellowships for the last two years.

My advisors, Professors Sheldon Blank and Matitiahu Tsevat, have been all that one could wish. When I was groping for an idea, or needed a word or phrase, I would go to Dr. Blank and say, "You know what I'm trying to say. Help me." And he did know. And he did help. And, it was not only for the paper that he had the right word. There were times when a personal word was needed. He had that word, too. Dr. Tsevat knows where to find things! The day after I spoke with him about the subject of this paper, a bibliography was on my desk. And, it was that way throughout. I'd say, "I've got a problem. It looks as though this is the solution, but . . ." If I was right, he told me where to go for support. When I was wrong, he was gentle.

Professor Elias Epstein, until recently Chairman of the Committee on Graduate Study, has been a willing and helpful counsellor.

Esther Kunkle has performed yeoman service with the typewriter. A maximum job in a minimum amount of time.

These people have been my father's allies. I am grateful to them and to him.

But, there are special people, and there are very special people. These days which should be the happiest of days are days of greatest sadness. As this is written, my mother lies just this side of death. When we visited together, a few days ago, we discussed the dedication of this dissertation. She agreed that what I had in mind was fitting, and thus it shall stand.

To my girls: Evelyn Brack Bergren
Sue Harman Bergren
Eva Lynn Bergren
Pamela Sue Bergren
Rebecca Anne Bergren

Cincinnati
April 7, 1972

ABBREVIATIONS

BASOR   Bulletin of the American Schools of Oriental
        Research

BDB   (Brown, Driver, and Briggs) <u>A Hebrew and English</u>
        <u>Lexicon of the Old Testament</u>

BH³   (R. Kittel, ed.) <u>Biblia Hebraica</u>. 3rd ed.

CBQ   Catholic Biblical Quarterly

GHAT   Göttinger Handkommentar zum Alten Testament

G-K   (E. Kautzsch, ed.) <u>Gesenius' Hebrew Grammar</u>

HTR   Harvard Theological Review

HUCA   Hebrew Union College Annual

IB   The Interpreter's Bible

IDB   The Interpreter's Dictionary of the Bible

JBL   Journal of Biblical Literature

JNES   Journal of Near Eastern Studies

LXX   Septuagint

MT   Massoretic Text

VT   Vetus Testamentum

ZAW   Zeitschrift für die alttestamentliche Wissenschaft

ZThK   Zeitschrift für Theologie und Kirche

THE PROPHETIC JUDGMENT-SPEECH (DAS PROPHETISCHE GERICHTSWORT)
AND ITS PARTS: ENGLISH AND GERMAN TERMS AND ABBREVIATIONS.[1]

Ac.   Accusation (Anklage)

An.   Announcement (Ankündigung)

AD   Announcement of Disaster (Unheilsankündigung)

AJ   Announcement of Judgment (Gerichtsankündigung)

CM   Commissioning of the Messenger (Botenauftrag)

GE   Das prophetische Gerichtswort an Einzelne = JI

GV   Die Gerichtsankündigung gegen Israel = JN

JI   Prophetic Judgment-Speech to Individuals = GE

JN   Announcement of Judgment against Israel = GV

MF   Messenger Formula (Botenformel)

MS   Messenger-Speech (Botenwort)

PJS   Prophetic Judgment-Speech

SH   Summons to Hear (Aufforderung zum Hören)

---

[1]We have adopted the form-critical terminology of Claus
Westermann, Grundformen Prophetischer Rede (München: Chr.
Kaiser Verlag, 1960).

INTRODUCTION

There is an old homiletic rule which reads: "Tell
them what you're going to tell them; then, tell them; and
finally, tell them what you've told them." When I received this rule, a reason came with it: "If they hear
it three times, they may remember it--repetition is an
aid to memory." While I have accepted the rule, my experience as parent (the rule is homiletic; the value,
pedagogic) has taught me that the reason is otherwise: if
you say it three times, your chances are that much greater
that they will hear it once.

In preaching and teaching I have adhered to this
method, albeit with a disquieting thought: is there "out
there" a paragon who, by superhuman effort, will deign to
listen all three times? Is there a way he may be encour-
aged to continue his admirable attentiveness? From these
questions, a methodological insight emerged. Why not let
your telling them what you're going to tell them take the
form of a presentation of the germination of an idea? This
way, the attentive listener will be able to see not only
where you are going, but what led you in that direction.

It is our intent to employ this procedure in the
present study, so that the reader may know not only where
we are going, but why we have begun the journey at all. Our
method will be to record what others have said and our

1

reactions to it. E. Hammershaimb has expressed our mood

precisely:

> Every Old Testament scholar has to found his results
> on whatever he inherited from his predecessors.
> Sometimes we accept uncritically or with sympathy the
> opinions of leading scholars, at other times we find
> ourselves in opposition thinking that the only way
> forward lies along new lines of research; but in all
> cases the research of the individual scholar is de-
> termined by its relation to our predecessors. The
> absolutely new only exists as a theoretical possibi-
> lity.[1]

Albrecht Alt, "Die Ursprünge des israelitischen Rechts,"
in Kleine Schriften zur Geschichte des Volkes Israels, I
(München: C. H. Beck'sche Verlagsbuchhandlung, 1953),
pp. 278-332.

In this 1934 monograph, Alt distinguished two streams

of law, examples of which are to be found in various places

in the Hexateuch, but which are found in conjunction in the

Book of the Covenant. Alt found the basic distinction to be

that casuistic law was formulated conditionally, while

apodictic law had a categorical formulation.

Casuistic law is recognized by the presence of the

following features: 1) it is introduced by a conditional

clause; 2) those involved in the case are referred to in

the third person; 3) in the protasis, the distinction be-

tween the main and subsidiary cases is expressed by two

different conjunctions, the stronger, "כי," "supposing

---

[1]E. Hammershaimb, "On the Ethics of the Old Testament
Prophets," Supplements to Vetus Testamentum, VII (Leiden:
E. J. Brill, 1960), p. 75.

that," and the weaker, "אם," "if" (pp. 286-7). Alt's ex-

ample is Ex. 21:18-19:

> Suppose that (כי) men quarrel and one strikes the
> other with a stone . . ., and the latter doesn't die
> but takes to his bed--if (אם) he gets up and walks
> outside upon his staff, then the assailant is clear-
> ed, he need only pay for his (the injured man's) in-
> capacitation and cure.

Such formal uniformity is lacking in apodictic law,

under which heading four main types are subsumed: 1) a

participial clause, describing a person's action, is fol-

lowed by a verbal predicate with infinitive absolute which

states the consequences of the action; the whole charac-

terized by a five-beat rhythm, e.g., Ex. 21:12, 15-17

(pp. 307-13); 2) a curse form, beginning with a passive

participle, e.g., Deut. 27:15-26 (pp. 313-15); 3) a series,

having an invariable verbal predicate with the negative

particle, the verb at the end of the sentence and the ob-

ject in the emphatic position, e.g., Lev. 18:7-17 (pp.

315-16); 4) the familiar Decalogue form of categorical

prohibition in the second person singular, e.g., Ex. 20:

3-17 (pp. 316-19). In spite of formal variations, what

unites these types is that all express a categorical pro-

hibition (p. 322).

Concomitant with this basic distinction, Alt finds

that each has a distinct _origin, outlook,_ and _Sitz im

Leben_: casuistic law is Canaanite in origin (pp. 295-96),

secular in outlook (p. 296), and has its setting in the

3

normal jurisdiction of the local courts (pp. 288-89); apodictic law, on the other hand, is related to the Israelite
people and the religion of Yahweh (p. 322), while its
life-situation is the covenant-renewal ceremony at the
Feast of Tabernacles where, every seventh year, it is proclaimed by the levitical priests (pp. 324-28).

The seminal nature of Alt's work is evidenced by the
number of studies for which it has served as springboard
and the controversy it has engendered; indeed, a proper
evaluation of these literary progeny would, itself, demand
a work of greater bulk than the original essay.[1] The effect
left by this scholarly activity is an impression of an
edifice whose pillars have been so severely damaged that the
entire structure is threatened with imminent destruction. A
sample of the critical undermining of Alt's position might
look like this:

---

[1]We list only those works to which we refer in our
summary of the major criticisms of Alt on the following
pages. The page numbers in parentheses on these pages refer
to the works here listed.
Erhard Gerstenberger, Wesen und Herkunft des sogenannten
apodiktischen Rechts im Alten Testament (Bonn: Rheinische
Friedrich-Wilhelms-Universität, 1961); George E. Menden-
hall, Law and Covenant in Israel and the Ancient Near East
(Pittsburgh: The Biblical Colloquium, 1955); Stanley
Gevirtz, "West-Semitic Curses and the Problem of the Ori-
gins of Hebrew Law," VT, XI (April, 1961), pp. 137-58;
Hammershaimb, "Ethics," pp. 75-101.
A convenient brief discussion of Alt's work and the deriv-
ative literature will be found in Eduard Nielsen's The Ten
Commandments in New Perspective (Naperville: Alec R.
Allenson, 1968), pp. 56-78.

1. Alt's category of apodictic law lacks formal cohesion;
there is need of a new grouping of Old Testament legal
materials. These points have been raised by Erhard Gerstenberger (pp. 33-35). He would distinguish between
". . . echte(n) Rechtssätze," which define the crime and
stipulate the legal consequences (such as Alt's apodictic,
participial construction of Ex. 21:12, 15-17) and prohibitions and commands, which do not stipulate the legal consequences (pp. 34-35).

2. Apodictic law is not uniquely Israelite. George Mendenhall has pointed to an occurrence of the Decalogue form
in one of the Hittite treaties (p. 7), while Stanley Gevirtz has noted the presence of apodictic formulations
among the West-Semitic curse inscriptions. Gevirtz's conclusion is:

> The uniqueness, if not the originality, in Israel of
> apodictic legal style, even that set in the second
> person singular, therefore, can no longer be upheld.[1]

3. The secular-religious distinction between casuistic
and apodictic law is untenable. Hammershaimb draws attention to Hammurabi's Law which, though casuistic in form,

> by its contents as well as by the relief on the stele
> on which his law is found, points to the law as some-
> thing sanctioned by the sun-god.[2]

---

[1]"Curses," p. 156.

[2]"Ethics," p. 79.

Gevirtz has pointed out that, in the Pentateuchal material, civil law can be found in apodictic form (e.g., Ex. 23:1-3), while ritual law can be set in casuistic style (e.g., Lev. 5:21 ff.).[1] Thus, another of Alt's neat distinctions apparently founders: non-Israelite law can have a religious orientation; and, apodictic law is not exclusively religious, nor casuistic law exclusively secular.

4. With respect to apodictic law, Alt has not seen that there is a difference between cultic _use_ and cultic _ori-gin_. The distinction is made by Gerstenberger in his consideration of "Die Sinaioffenbarung" (pp. 81-82). Gerstenberger's own thesis is that the _origin_ of the prohibitions is to be associated with the clan (pp. 95-100).

At this point, it is not our intent to engage in the usual practice of rebutting the rebutters, but to inquire after the condition of Alt's edifice. For some reason, while reading the varied criticisms of Alt's position we were reminded of a fellow with whom we used to play tennis. He had an abominable serve; could not hit a proper backhand; never came to the net; but, one way or another, he would _keep getting the ball back_. That is, while the pillars of his game were non-existent, in the significant matter of keeping the ball in play his game was unassailably sound.

---

[1]"Curses," p. 156, fn. 2.

Just so, did the question begin to emerge in relation to
Alt's work: had he, in a similarly mystifying way, got the
point of it all? It was at this time that we happened to
turn to . . .

Claus Westermann, Grundformen Prophetischer Rede (München:
Chr. Kaiser Verlag, 1960).

In his "Preface to the English Edition" of this work,
Westermann apparently recognizes that the title is a mis-
nomer because here he defines more narrowly the extent of
his treatment:

> In the investigation presented here not all prophetic
> utterances are examined, but only the judgment-
> speeches to individuals, those to Israel, and other
> forms related to them.[1]

Westermann is, throughout the investigation, the
practitioner of form criticism: 1) He delineates the
purest form of the PJS;[2] 2) He indicates the development
of the form; 3) He ascertains its "Sitz im Leben."

1. The pristine form of the PJS is to be found in the JI.
While it may be introduced by the CM or the SH; the invariable components are the Ac., the MF, and the An., in that

---

[1]Basic Forms of Prophetic Speech, trans. by Hugh
Clayton White (Philadelphia: The Westminster Press, 1967),
p. 12.

[2]For the abbreviations which will be used throughout this paper to designate the Prophetic Judgment-Speech
and its parts, see p. vii. Except in direct quotations
from Westermann, we will prefer the English terms and abbreviations.

7

<u>order</u>. I Kings 21:19 is an example:[1]

Accusation:[2]   "Have you committed murder, and also taken possession?"

Messenger Formula: "Thus says the Lord:

Announcement: In the place where the dogs lapped Naboth's blood will dogs lap your blood--yes, yours."

While Westermann takes note of a number of formal characteristics, from other places in his book it is clear that, with regard to the form, three things are given special emphasis:

a. The formal unity of the Ac. and the An.:

Das GE ist zweiteilig; es enthält eine Anklage und eine Ankündigung. Erst beide zusammen machen das Botenwort aus; beide haben ihre Existenz nur als Glied eines Ganzen.[3]

b. That the Ac. serves as reason for the An.:

Will man diesen Teil (i.e., the Ac.) des Prophetenwortes <u>als Teil</u>, d. h. in seiner Funktion für das prophetische Gerichtswort als Ganzes bezeichnen, so genügt durchaus die formale Bezeichnung "Begründung"; will man aber ausdrücken, worin diese Begründung besteht, was sie, für sich genommen, darstellt,

---

[1]The complete form is set out by Westermann along with additional examples in <u>Grundformen</u>, p. 93.

[2]In the form of an accusing question. For a discussion of the forms taken by the Accusation, see <u>Ibid.</u>, pp. 102-05.

[3]<u>Ibid.</u>, p. 94. Westermann explains his choice of the designations "Ac." and "An." in an excursus on pp. 46-49.

so ist die sachgemässe Bezeichnung "Anklage."[1]

c.   That the MS proper comprises only the An.:

> . ... Gotteswort im eigentlichen Sinn ist nur die
> Ankündigung; sie ist als solche durch die sie ein-
> leitende Botenformel (mit "darum") gekennzeichnet,
> die Anklage steht vor dem eigentlichen Botenwort.[2]

2.   When, in the literary prophets, the PJS comes to be
directed against the nation (Westermann makes the pertinent observation that what begins with Amos is not judgment prophecy as such, but rather the JN),[3] a corresponding formal development takes place (p. 120). In the JN,
both the Ac. and the An. are divided into two parts (pp.
121-22). The MF likewise undergoes modification, being
abbreviated, omitted, or undergoing a change of position
(p. 129). In Jeremiah, and throughout Ezekiel, the MF appears at the beginning of the speech, "damit ist das ganze
Prophetenwort als Gotteswort gekennzeichnet" (p. 129).
Westermann concludes his chapter on the JN with a formal
discussion of the "Wehe-Ruf" (Cry of Woe), a variant of the

---

[1]Ibid., p. 49.

[2]Ibid., p. 94. When this and the quotation before
last are read together (they are from the same paragraph
in the text), it will be seen that there is some confusion
as to what does constitute "das Botenwort"; the An. alone,
or the Ac. and the An. We attempt to explain the reason
for this confusion in a brief excursus on p. 23.

[3]Ibid., p. 99.

PJS (pp. 137-42), and of some other forms in which prophetic speech may be clothed; among them, "Die Rechts-
verhandlung" (Legal Procedure) (pp. 143-44), and "Die
Klage" (Lament) (pp. 145-46).

Westermann's study of the formal development of the
PJS is of value in two ways. First, he who wishes to
study this speech form (other than in terms of its form)
has the texts isolated for him. Second, since one of the
most difficult tasks confronting the biblical student is
that of defining the limits of a particular prophetic
speech, Westermann's formal canon that the real unit of the
PJS consists of Ac. plus AD is a significant aid.

Westermann's discussion of "expansions" of the parts
and framework of the PJS (pp. 130-36) is also of moment
with regard to the problem of delimitation. We will let
one example suffice. In the PJS in Amos 2:6-16 and in the
"lawsuit" in Jer. 2:1-13 are to be found references to the
saving acts of God in history (p. 131). Are these references, which Westermann terms expansions of the Ac. to be
thought of as secondary? By no means:

> Doch dürfen die Erweiterungen als solche keines-
> falls als sekundär angesehen werden; vielmehr ent-
> halten besonders bei den Propheten des 8. Jahr-
> hunderts gerade diese nicht unmittelbar zur Struk-
> tur des Gerichtswortes gehörenden Erweiterungen
> oft das dem betreffenden Propheten Eigenste.[1]

---

[1]Ibid., p. 130.

This formal criterion has an impact on the <u>content</u> of the Judgment-Speech. The Ac. is now given dimension. Amos and Jeremiah are no longer saying, "This is what you have done"; but, "Look what you have done, in spite of what God has done for you!"

3. It is Westermann's contention that the PJS has a juridical "Sitz im Leben." The battle is joined on two fronts: a denial of a cultic setting and an affirmation of a judicial one.

a. In his discussion of Würthwein's, "Der Ursprung der prophetischen Gerichtsrede"[1] (pp. 54-57), Westermann encounters the view that the origin of the PJS is to be sought in a cultic event in which Yahweh appears as judge (p. 55). His argument is to say to Würthwein, "You can't have it both ways." In an earlier work, "Amos-Studien,"[2] Würthwein had made two points with which Westermann is in total agreement: that the PJS is to be perceived "als Ganzheit in seinen zwei Teilen: Unheilsankündigung und . . . die Anklage . . ." (p. 55); and

> . . . dass die Worte des Kult- oder Heilsnabi Amos
> deutlich und unmissverständlich zu unterscheiden
> sind von den Worten des Unheilspropheten Amos . . .[3]

---

[1]<u>ZThK</u>, 49 (1952), pp. 1-15.

[2]<u>ZAW</u>, 62 (1950), pp. 10-52.

[3]<u>Grundformen</u>, pp. 56-57.

Now, however, in attempting to tie the PJS to a cultic event,
Würthwein gives evidence of formal inconsistency by taking
into consideration only the Ac. (Würthwein uses the term
"Scheltwort"), treating it as an independent speech-form
(pp. 55-56). Further, having demonstrated in his earlier
work that the concern of the cult-prophet is to effect
salvation, Würthwein now wishes to give the PJS a cultic
orientation (pp. 56-57). For Westermann, then, the results
which Würthwein had achieved in his "Amos-Studien," have
invalidated the thesis advanced in his more recent work.
b. Westermann's own argument for a judicial setting for
the PJS is to be found in his discussion of the JI (pp.
95-98). It consists of a mixture of formal insights with
observations as to content.

Let us again set out Elijah's speech to Ahab:

Accusation: "Have you committed murder, and
                                also taken possession?"

Messenger Formula: "Thus says the Lord:

Announcement: In the place where the dogs lap-
                                ped Naboth's blood will dogs lap
                                your blood--yes, yours."

In this speech, says Westermann, four things happen which
correspond to regular judicial procedure: 1) the accused
is an individual; 2) who has just transgressed (according
to the Ac.); 3) a current law in Israel; 4) and, the An.
corresponds to a decision announced by the court (pp. 95-96).
Further, not only is there an apparent correspondence to

12

actual judicial procedure; but, our example shows a __formal__
correspondence to ancient Israelite law, which a comparison
with Ex. 21:12 illustrates:

Whoever strikes a man mortally, shall be put to death.
In each (the PJS and the legal maxim), there is a division
into two basic elements: first, an offense; then, the proceedings which are to emanate therefrom (p. 97).

Cult, or court? In which is the origin of the PJS
to be found? Westermann's conclusion is:

> Dann ist--jedenfalls für das prophetische Gerichts-
> wort an einen einzelnen--die Annahme seiner Herkunft
> aus einem kultischen Gerichtsakt nicht nötig. Die
> Nähe zum ordentlichen Gerichtsverfahren und zum alt-
> en Gottesrecht ist offenkundig.[1]

In the process of characterizing the JI and arguing
for its judicial setting, Westermann makes some observations bearing upon its "Sitz im Leben"--"Sitz im Leben"
understood now, not in its usual formal sense, but in what
we might call a functional sense; i.e., observations which
might answer questions such as, "What situation gives rise
to the JI?" or, "Why is there a JI at all?" To think along
with Westermann at this point, it is well to go back to the
speech of Elijah in I Kings 21:19 and reflect upon the
__position__ of the person to whom it is directed. That's right,
__king__ Ahab. Now, says Westermann, when a king commits a

---

[1]__Ibid.__, p. 97.

13

crime, there is no higher authority capable of intervening
(pp. 93-94).

> Da aber schreitet Gott selbst ein. Er tut es,
> indem er einen Boten, den Propheten Elia, beauf-
> tragt, dem König entgegenzutreten, ihn auf seine
> Tat hin zu stellen und ihm das Gerichtsurteil Gott-
> es anzukündigen.[1]

Further, since in normal judicial procedure the decision
would be rendered by a court ("Das ist hier nicht möglich,
weil niemand da ist, der eine solche Gerichtsversammlung
gegen den König einberuft"), God takes the place of the
court--appearing as judge (p. 96). In relation to this,
the prophet has a clearly-defined task:

> Der Prophet hat dem Angeklagten dieses Urteil Gottes
> zu übermitteln, er ist der Bote, der das von Gott
> gesprochene Urteil vor den Angeklagten--in diesem
> Fall den König--trägt und es ihm verkündet.[2]

To summarize: The JI fills a gap. In any society, there
are those who are exempt from the punishment which justice
requires. Westermann's point is that, in Israelite society, for a limited period of time, God remedied this situation by sending a messenger, the prophet, whose instru-
ment was the JI.

However, if the prophet is messenger, and his in-

---

[1]Ibid., p. 94. Westermann declares a similar motivation ". . . bei den Wehe-Worten der Propheten des 8.
Jahrhunderts . . ."--without which, ". . . die darin ge-
troffene Tat unbestraft bliebe" (p. 142).

[2]Ibid., p. 96.

strument the JI, this implies that the JI is a Messenger-Speech (MS). And so, says Westermann, it is. To be precise, it is Westermann's thesis that the PJS, which comprises both the JI and the JN, is a MS. To this matter, we must now turn.

In the summary of his review of previous research into prophetic speech-forms (pp. 7-57), Westermann indicates the direction his own inquiry will take:

> An diese neue Bestimmung des prophetischen Gerichtswortes als Botenwort in den beiden Teilen Begründung und Ankündigung muss nach meinem Verständnis die weitere Erarbeitung der prophetischen Redeformen anschliessen.[1]

This leads to a consideration of "Das prophetische Wort als Botenwort" (pp. 70-91), in which Westermann does five things.

1. He sets out the form of the MS, of which Gen. 45:9 may serve as our example:[2]

Commissioning of the Messenger:	Hurry along to my father and say to him,
Messenger Formula:	"Thus says your son, Joseph,
Messenger-Speech: Report:	God has made me lord of all Egypt;

---

[1]Ibid., p. 61.

[2]The complete form, as set out by Westermann (p. 72), is more elaborate. Our example includes only those features necessary to present his argument for the MS character of the PJS.

Summons: Please come down to me with-
                            out delay."

The message, itself, consists of two parts; a report (in
the perfect) and a summons (in the imperative). The report tends to serve as a reason for the summons (pp. 75-76).
2. He declares that an ordinary speech, in becoming a
message, "nimmt als Botschaft bestimmte, feste Formen an,
die es erst zur Botschaft machen" (p. 79). That is, one
cannot, by simply placing "thus says . . ." before a
speech, make it a MS. The speech delivered by messengers
to Ahab in I Kings 20:3 is an example:

> Thus says Benhadad:
> "Your silver and gold are mine;
> your choicest wives and children are mine."

This, Westermann would call an ultimatum, rather than a
message (p. 78).
3. He distinguishes the message from a command (ultimatum,
proclamation). The conjunction of two features characterizes
a message: it consists of a perfect and an imperative part
(cp. Benhadad's ultimatum to Ahab), and it offers a decision
(Entscheidung) to the addressee (p. 79).
4. He wonders how a speech which requires directness can
become a MS, and offers the example of a diplomatic negotiation (a speech which does require directness) which,
in Judges 11:12-27, is presented in the form of a MS. The
features to be noted are:
a. The occasion of the message is a misdeed of the ad-

16

dressee (p. 80):

> Then Jephthah sent messengers to the king of the
> Ammonites to say, "What's the trouble between us
> that you have come to me to fight against my land?"
> (11:12)

There is, here, a formal correspondence to the PJS to

Israel, which is ". . . ausgelöst durch eine Verfehlung

Israels" (p. 81).

b. The message has the character of an Ac. (in the form of

an accusing question), and indicates . . .

> . . . in welchem Zusammenhang eine anklagende Frage
> . . . zum Teil einer Botschaft werden kann: wenn
> eine Verfehlung vorliegt und der, an dem sie geschah,
> die Entfernten durch einen Boten nach dem Rechtsgrund
> ihres Verhaltens fragt.[1]

c. The essential content of Jephthah's message (11:14-27)

may be reduced to: "Ihr habt keinen Grund, uns anzu-

fallen, euer Einfall ist ein Vergehen. Jetzt werden die

Waffen sprechen." This corresponds to the two-part message

in the PJS: Reason and Announcement (p. 81).

What Westermann seems to be saying is that here (in

Judges 11:12-27), in what is clearly a MS, the elements

of a PJS (which is also occasioned by a misdeed of the ad-

dressee; and which consists of an Ac. and An., the former

serving as reason for the latter) are to be found.

5. He presents a summary of the preliminary results ob-

tained from an analysis of the linguistic structure of the

---

[1]Grundformen, p. 81.

Mari texts in comparison with prophetic speech-forms in the
Old Testament (pp. 84-91). His conclusion is that the Mari
texts confirm the ". . . Charkter der Prophetensprüche als
Botensprüche . . ." (p. 91). In the course of his analysis,
Westermann makes a special point of the position which (in
one of the letters) those sentences occupy which serve to
identify the word of God: they come ". . . nach den Sätzen,
die einen Vorwurf gegen den König enthalten . . . (and) vor
den Sätzen, die die eigentliche Gottesbotschaft enthalten
. . ." (p. 86). That is, there is a formal similarity to
the PJS, in which the MF stands after the Ac. and before the
An., thereby designating the latter as the real word of God
(p. 86).

These five observations, which we have now summarized,
are, apparently, Westermann's attempt to demonstrate the
validity of his insight that the PJS is to be defined as a
MS, consisting of two parts, Reason and An. Does this, in
fact, amount to a demonstration? If we were to attempt to
encapsulate Westermann's observations on "Das prophetische
Wort als Botenwort," it would be in this vein: after
setting out the form of and criteria for determining a MS,
he goes on to examine some Messenger-Speeches (the diplomatic negotiation of Judges 11:12-27 and the Mari letters)
which have formal variations from and/or do not conform to
the criteria established for determining a MS; which

deviations, moreover, are to be found also in the PJS. That
is, bona fide Messenger-Speeches deviate from the MS at
precisely the same points as does the PJS. Necessary conclusion: since these are, despite the deviations, bona fide
Messenger-Speeches, so, too, may be the PJS!) These deviations are:

1. While in the MS the MF precedes the two-part speech
(cp. p. 15, above), in one of the Mari letters, the functional equivalent of the MF comes in the middle, between
the two parts (p. 86; cp. p. 18, above). This corresponds
to the position of the MF in the PJS (cp. p. 7, above).

2. The MS consists of a perfect and an imperative part
(cp. p. 16, above). However, in Jephthah's reply, through
messengers, to the Ammonites (Judges 11:27), ". . . An
der Stelle des imperativischen Teils steht hier etwas ganz
anderes, eine Ankündigung . . ." (p. 80). This, too, one
finds to be the case in the PJS (cp. p. 7, above; note that
both I Kings 21:19 and Judges 11:27 have the imperfect).

3. There is a third deviation which Westermann does not
note, and which is to be found in the MS in Judges 11. While
a criterion of the MS is that it offers a decision to the
addressee (cp. p. 16, above), the An. of Judges 11:27
declares the irrevocable decision of the sender of the message in relation to the addressee. This deviation is also
characteristic of the An. in the PJS (cp. p. 12, above).

Focusing, for the moment, on the second and third deviations, we may formulate our criticism of Westermann in the following way: if the effective criteria of a MS (as opposed, e.g., to an ultimatum or a royal proclamation) are that it contains a perfect and an imperative part and that it offers a decision to the addressee (cp. p. 16, above), then the PJS (along with the diplomatic negotiation of Judges 11 and the Mari letter) cannot be a MS since it defaults in respect to these criteria, no matter what features it may hold in common with the MS.[1]

---

[1]In "Botenformel und Botenspruch," ZAW (1962), pp. 165-77, Rolf Rendtorff denies a formal relationship between prophetic speech and the MS. He argues in two steps. He contends: 1) that an examination of several Messenger-Speeches in the Pentateuch and historical books shows that the MF is not so indissolubly linked to the MS that, from the prophets' use of the MF, the taking over of the form of the MS must be assumed (pp. 166-69); and 2) that the MS has no uniform formal characteristics (pp. 169-72), so that, for example, that some Messenger-Speeches and the PJS have two parts is simply a matter of chance (p. 174). The first point does not tell against Westermann, for he argues that a message has, itself, a definite form, independent of the MF (see p. 16, above). The second point is one of basic disagreement. Westermann would call the one-word speech in I Kings 2:30--which Rendtorff calls a MS, and from which he argues that the MS has no uniform formal characteristics (p. 169)--not a message, but a command (cp. p. 16, above). Our own feeling is that Westermann is correct in that the normal MS does have two parts, while Rendtorff is correct "dass die Form des Botenwortes entscheidend bestimmt ist durch die jeweilige Situation" (p. 169).

While Rendtorff denies a formal relationship between prophetic speech and the MS, he feels that certain stylistic elements of prophetic speech (the prophets speak in the I-form of Yahweh and use הנני followed by a participle in announcing an approaching act of Yahweh) do exhibit influence by the MS (pp. 176-77).

However, given Westermann's contention that the PJS has a juridical "Sitz im Leben," (cp. pp. 8-11, above), one might still argue for the MS character of the PJS in a different way.

In any MS there is, inevitably, a tension between the MS _form_ and the _content_ of that which is to be transmitted. Insofar as possible, the latter will conform itself to the former; where it cannot do so, the MS form must make the accommodation. Such accommodation is evident in Judges 11. In the reply of the king of the Ammonites to Jephthah (11:13), the MS form (perfect followed by imperative offering a decision to the addressee) is patent. In Jephthah's reply (11:27), however, which puts an end to negotiation, the imperative gives way to an An. which uses the imperfect to convey to the Ammonites Jephthah's intent to fight. That is, while the diplomatic negotiation accomodated itself nicely to the MS form, Jephthah's resolution to fight did not, and it was the MS form which was forced to give way.

The situation is similar with regard to the PJS. In the PJS, there is a tension between its form as a MS and the juridical setting of its content. _It is this tension which accounts for the deviations_ we have noted.

1. In a trial, there is an Ac. and an AJ; but, only the latter is spoken by the judge. In the PJS, this aspect of regular judicial procedure is reflected in the position

21

occupied by the MF--just prior to the An.--as opposed to its
position in the MS. The effect of this influence of the
juridical setting is that, in the PJS, only the An. is to be
understood as the word of the sender of the message (i.e.,
God).

2. In the MS form, the intent of the message (i.e., to get
the addressee to do something) is underlined by the form
taken by the verb, the imperative. In a trial, the AJ
states what is to happen to the addressee "from this time
forth . . ."; for which, the imperfect (the future in
English) is the proper verbal form (e.g., "you will go to
prison"). Here also, then, the juridical setting exerts its
influence on the MS form--in the PJS, the An. will have the
verb in the imperfect (plus לא).

3. Similarly, in a trial, when the judge announces sentence,
he declares the "will of the court" in relation to the
defendant--there is no question of presenting the defendant
with an option. Once again, the PJS carries over the
judicial setting at the expense of the MS form.

Thus, the PJS may be understood as a MS; since, 1)
the PJS is formally similar to the MS (see the excursus below), and 2) the deviations from this form are explicable
by reference to the juridical setting of the PJS.

Excursus: The Formal Similarity of the MS and the PJS.

22

Let us set side by side the examples of the MS and
the PJS:

MS (Gen. 45:9)   PJS (I Kings 21:18-19)

Hurry along to my father   CM   . . . go along down to
and say to him,   meet Ahab . . . and say
                                 to him,

"Thus says your son,   MF   -----[1]
Joseph,

God has made me lord of   (1) "Have you committed mur-
all Egypt;   der, and also taken pos-
                                 session?"

-----   MF   "Thus says the Lord:

Please come down to me   (2) In the place where the
without delay."   dogs lapped Naboth's blood
                                 will dogs lap your blood--
                                 yes, yours,"

Both speech forms: 1) begin with the CM; 2) have a MF; 3)
have a two-part speech, in which the first part tends to
serve as reason for the second. The elements of divergence
between the two forms have been noted above with an attempted explanation of these divergences (cp. pp. 18-22).

Excursus: A Conundrum.

_____

[1]The usual form of the PJS has the MF after part 1.
I Kings 21:18-19 has the MF both before and after. We have
followed Westermann in omitting the first occurrence. He
explains: "Zum Text von 1. Reg. 21, 17-19 ist anzumerken,
dass die Einleitungsformeln in der Überlieferung des Textes
ganz unsicher sind. Dass die Botenformel bei einem so
frühen und so kurzen Wort zweimal stand . . ., ist ganz
unwahrscheinlich. Das erste, 'so sprach Jahwe' in 19a ist
zu streichen . . ." (p. 94, fn. 1).

Find the MS in the PJS outlined in the preceding
paragraph, remembering that: 1) a MS has two parts; and 2)
the MS is that which follows the MF (cp. the MS form in the
preceding paragraph). When this formal dilemma is posed,
one is better placed to understand Westermann's apparently
pedantic distinction between a "Botenwort" and an "eigentlichen Botenwort":

> Das GE ist zweiteilig; es enthält eine Anklage und
> eine Ankündigung. Erst beide zusammen machen das
> Botenwort aus; beide haben ihre Existenz nur als
> Glied eines Ganzen. „Aber Gotteswort im eigentlichen
> Sinn ist nur die Ankündigung; sie ist als solche
> durch die sie einleitende Botenformel (mit 'darum')
> gekennzeichnet, die Anklage steht vor dem eigentlich-
> en Botenwort.[1]

This distinction is the way in which Westermann resolves
the conundrum set out above: 1) the two parts (which
every MS must have) have been isolated--therefore, the PJS
is a MS ("Botenwort"); 2) the MS ("eigentlichen Botenwort")
does follow the MF. Whether or not we like his solution,
at least we can appreciate the problem.

Excursus: The Word of God and the Word of the Prophet.

The position of the MF (in the PJS) between the two
parts of the MS leads Westermann to the observation:

> Nur die Ankündigung des Gerichts ist--streng genommen
> --das ihm offenbarte Gotteswort, das er weiterzugeben

---

[1]Grundformen, p. 94.

hat. In der Begründung spricht der Prophet selber.[1]

This distinction between the AJ as the word of God and the Ac. as the word of the prophet receives confirmation from Koch's scrutiny of the speech of Elijah in II Kings 1. The speech is reported three times (vss. 3-4, 7, and 16); and, while the wording of the Ac. is changed each time, the AJ remains unchanged. The implication of this freedom in reporting the Ac. is that

> The prophetic guilds, which transmitted such legends and sayings, would not have understood the prophet's diatribe (i.e., the Ac.) to be verbally inspired, but merely as the prophet's own words.[2]

Thus Westermann's conclusion from the form-critical evidence

---

[1]Ibid., p. 53. Cp. also the passage to which the previous fn. refers: ". . . Gotteswort im eigentlichen Sinn ist nur die Ankündigung . . ." The reader of Westermann is subject to the same kind of confusion with respect to his use of the phrase "word of God" as we saw to be the case with "Botenwort." Whereas in the passages here quoted he is at pains to define the "announcement" as "Gotteswort," in his discussion on pp. 66-67 he states that the prophetic books identify all the words of the prophets with the word of God. It seems to me that the difficulty stems from the tension between theological presupposition (the prophetic word is the word of God) and form-critical observation (only the "announcement" is designated as the word of God). Westermann, of course, would argue that the presupposition is the Bible's, not his (pp. 66-67). His resolution of this semantic dilemma is the same as we noted with respect to the "Botenwort" dilemma. He uses the word "eigentlich": "Gotteswort im eigentlichen Sinn ist nur die Ankündigung."

[2]Klaus Koch, The Growth of the Biblical Tradition, trans. by S. M. Cupitt (New York: Charles Scribner's Sons, 1969), p. 192. Koch's discussion will be found on pp. 191-193.

is buttressed by Koch's observation of a change in content.
The problem is that the MF has a way of jumping around (in
II Kings 1:3-4 it is between the Ac. and the AJ, while in
vss. 7 and 16 it precedes both elements), and, in the later
prophets (cp. p. 9, above), appears characteristically at
the beginning of the speech. Nevertheless, time has a way
of dissolving forms and blurring distinctions, and this
would seem to be the case here. We would agree with
Westermann that the original form of the PJS witnesses to an
original distinction between the Ac. as the word of the
prophet and the AJ as the word of God.

While Westermann's insights into the form and setting
of the PJS will be of considerable value to us later when
we shall be dealing directly with many such speeches, it is
certain other things which arose in our reading of Wes-
termann--things which evoked in us the intent to pursue
them further--that here claim our attention.

1. The Content of the PJS: Westermann and Alt.

Alt distinguished between apodictic and casuistic law;
Westermann, in his study of the PJS, finds occasion to
allude to the former, in one case even using the term. He
points out that the Ac. portion of the PJS may take either
of two forms: accusing question (pp. 102-04), or declaratory sentence (pp. 104-06). In discussing the declaratory
sentence, he observes:

26

Diese lapidaren, feststellenden Sätze der Anklage
sind den apodiktischen Geboten genau entsprechend:
auch diese in der 2. pers. sing. formuliert, jedoch
als Verbote im imperf. mit lo'.[1]

Further on, in his discussion of the Accusation portion of

the "Wehe-Ruf," a variant of the PJS, Westermann comments:

(Dazu kommt, dass) es sich in allen diesen Wehe-
Worten um soziale Anklage handelt. (Wieder) liege
die Frage nahe, ob hier nicht eine Beziehung zu
Fluchsprüchen vorliegen könnte, die ja stilistisch
auffällig ähnlich sind:

Verflucht   der Schlagende seinen Nachbarn im Geheim-
             en! (Dtn. 27, 24)
Wehe   die Herbeiziehenden die Sünde mit Strick-
             en! (Jes. 5, 18 ff.)

Auch die Fluchworte in Dtn. 27 haben es ausschliess-
lich mit dem Zusammenleben der Gemeinschaft zu tun.[2]

Remembering that the curse is, according to Alt (cp. p. 3,

above), one of the forms taken by apodictic law, one is

here apprised, not only of a formal correspondence of the

Ac. to apodictic law, but of a similarity in content (both

the Ac. in the "Wehe-Ruf" and the curse have a social ref-

erence). Is this similarity in content limited only to

the "Wehe-Ruf" and the curse, and only to their having a

common domain of concern? No, indeed!

In his discussion of the structure of the JI (pp.

93-98), Westermann leaves the matter of its formal char-

acteristics to look at the content of two of his examples

---

[1]Grundformen, p. 105.

[2]Ibid., p. 139.

27

(I Kings 21:18-19 and II Kings 1:3-4), and remarks:

> In beiden Fällen ist das Vergehen der Bruch eines alt-
> en Gottesrechtes: Ahab (i. Reg. 21) hat gegen das
> Verbot des Tötens (Ex. 21, 12), Ahasja (2. Reg. 1)
> gegen das Verbot, sich an andere Götter zu wenden (Ex.
> 23, 13) gehandelt.[1]

While one would not wish to dispute Westermann's
statement that the laws of Ex. 21:12 and 23:13 are "old
laws of God," the reader who has Alt on his mind cannot
help but note that both laws belong formally to the category of apodictic law. And here, the connection between
the PJS (specifically, the Ac.) and apodictic law extends
beyond form to content: in two cases, a prophet accuses
a king of the breach of a law which, in the Bible, appears
in apodictic form. Is this mere chance, or did the breach
of those laws which Alt called apodictic--and only those
laws--evoke prophetic response? If one were to read Alt's
apodictic laws for their content, and the Ac. portions of
Prophetic Judgment-Speeches for their content, would one
find other cases where apodictic law apparently stood behind prophetic Ac.? Westermann's remarks generate enough
smoke that an investigation of the content of the PJS in the
light of Alt's legal categories seems worthy of pursuit.

2. The Context of the PJS.

Having summarized the contributions of Würthwein's

---

[1]Ibid., p. 95.

"Amos-Studien" which are of relevance for his own inquiry
(among them, that Amos accuses his people of transgressing
not moral law, but the law of God), Westermann goes on to
say:

> . . . prophetische Anklage ist damit als ein nur aus
> einer bestimmten einmaligen Geschichte verständlich-
> er, auf dieser Geschichte beruhender Vorgang erwies-
> en. . . . (sie ist) mit der vorangehenden Epoche
> verkettet und ohne sie nicht zu verstehen: mit dem
> 'Bund', dessen eine Seite Gottes Erwahlung, dessen
> andere Seite die Verpflichtung dieses Bundes für das
> Volk war.[1]

That is, in the PJS, we are dealing not with an isolated
event, but with something whose meaning is discernible only in the larger context of the previous relationship between God and people. (Or, to say it differently, an event
may have a meaning in itself, and an additional meaning which
is only revealed by its context. If I put my arm around my
daughter, it is a sign of parental affection. If this was
done after I had disciplined her, it is a sign of forgive-
ness as well.) Are there hints within the speeches themselves which point to this larger context? The expanded
Ac., where the Ac. is set against the background of the deeds
of God (cp. Westermann's discussion, pp. 131-32) is one such
pointer. Does the PJS contain other indications of the
larger context which illumines its meaning?
Robert Bach, "Gottesrecht und weltliches Recht in der

---

[1]Ibid., p. 53.

29

Verkündigung des Propheten Amos," in Festschrift für Gün-
ther Dehn (Neukirchen: 1957), pp. 23-34.

While this essay appeared three years before Westermann's Grundformen, it came to our attention only after
we had read Westermann and been struck by the affinity of
prophetic accusation to apodictic law.

It is Bach's intent

> . . . die Überlieferungen, die in der Verkündigung
> des Propheten Amos aufgegriffen werden, an einem
> Punkte etwas genauer zu bestimmen, . . .[1]

Bach begins by accepting Alt's distinction between apodictic and casuistic law, notes the association of these two
types of law in the Book of the Covenant and Deuteronomy,
and wonders whether their conjunction corresponds to an
"einmal üblich gewesenen Rechtspraxis" or is a purely literary work. Were the latter the case, then the possibility would exist

> . . . dass die beiden Rechtsgattungen zur Zeit des
> Amos ihr Eigenleben noch nicht aufgegeben hatten,
> . . .

and it would be proper to attempt

> . . . die Rechtstradition, an die Amos in seiner
> Verkündigung anknüpft, noch genauer zu bestimmen.[2]

Bach's method is to focus upon that part of Amos' message

---

[1]"Gottesrecht," p. 23.

[2]Bach's argument, summarized in this paragraph, is
to be found on pp. 24-25. The quotations are from p. 25.

which attempts to substantiate (begründen) the disaster
which the prophet announces (what Westermann calls the Ac.)
and to ask whether Amos, in his accusations, makes reference
to both forms of Israelite law or only to one of them
(p. 25). His conclusion is that Amos refers only to apodictic law and that, therefore, the old dualism between the two
laws had not been overcome by the prophet's time (p. 33).

   Bach does, with one prophet, what our reading of
Westermann in the light of Alt had suggested (cp. p. 28,
above). In so doing, he shows that Alt and Amos were,
apparently, on the same wave-length. Alt recognized an A
group of laws (apodictic) and a B group of laws (casuistic);
and, says Bach, Amos did too--evidenced by the fact that his
preaching of judgment refers only to the A group. Bach's
essay confirms our intent to explore the possibility of a
connection between apodictic law and prophetic accusation.

   But, should there prove to be such a connection, how
is it to be explained? In his concluding paragraph, Bach
(following Würthwein and Noth) remarks that the proclamation
of Amos is based on ". . . den Bund Jahwes mit Israel"
(p. 34), and continues:

> Diese Bezogenheit der Unheilsverkündigung des Amos
> auf den Bund Jahwes mit Israel wird noch deutlich-
> er, wenn Amos wirklich nur das auf den Bund be-
> zogene apodiktische und nicht auch das ganz anders
> geartete kasuistische Recht zum Massstab der Be-

31

gründungen seiner Unheilsankündigungen macht.[1]
We have already quoted Westermann's statement that covenant
is a key to understanding prophetic accusation (p. 29,
above); now Bach asserts that apodictic law and Amos' proclamation of disaster are covenant-related.

George E. Mendenhall, Law and Covenant in Israel and the
Ancient Near East (Pittsburgh: The Biblical Colloquium,
1955).

This study is divided into two parts. In the first
section (pp. 3-23), Mendenhall distinguishes between legal
"policy" and legal "techniques," and looks at the Decalogue
and Covenant Code in the light of this distinction.
"Policy" is "that common body of what might be called the
sense of justice in a community"; while "techniques" designate "the technical corpus of specialized legal acts and
traditions . . . whereby the generally vague community con-
cepts of justice are translated into action in the specific
cases which come before the judges" (p. 3).

The Decalogue is an example of legal "policy." At
Sinai, there emerged a people bound together by covenant
"in a religious and political community." The Decalogue
was the text of that covenant, ". . . the stipulation of the
obligations to the deity which the community accepted as
binding" (p. 5). Since, however, breach of covenant by a

---

[1]Ibid., p. 34.

32

member of the community brings upon it the divine wrath, the community must dissociate itself from an offender.[1] The techniques by which it accomplishes this dissociation are law (in the proper sense) (pp. 5-6).

While neither in the Ancient Near East in general nor in Israel prior to the Exile in particular were there collections of laws which _functioned_ _as_ legislation in the sense of an authoriatative "written lawcode" which, by means of interpretation and application, was used by judges to arrive at a decision (p. 9), the Covenant Code represents some steps beyond the Decalogue in this direction. First, in addition to "policy," it contains examples of "techniques" in the form of case law (p. 14). Second, even the material in apodictic form is "more concrete" than the stipulations of the Decalogue; and, in providing for punishment, adds legal sanctions to what, in the Decalogue, was simply "policy" (p. 15). Ex. 21:15 illustrates the second point:

> Whoever strikes his father or mother shall be put to death.

The Decalogue stipulation, "Honor your father and mother" (Ex. 20:12a), is here given a "fer instance," and the

---

[1]Mendenhall points to Joshua 7, II Sam. 24:12-14, and Jonah 1:11-12 as examples of a community suffering for the misdeed of an individual (p. 4, fn. 6).

33

punishment for disobedience is designated.[1] Thus, while
the Covenant Code "is (still) actually a description of
legal policy (it is) much more specific than the original
foundation of the Decalogue . . ." (p. 17).

When one thinks about the Covenant Code and apodictic
and casuistic law, one cannot help but think also about
Albrecht Alt; and Mendenhall is no exception. In particular,
he is concerned with Alt's view that apodictic law has an
Israelite, and casuistic law a Canaanite provenance. In
regard to the former point, Mendenhall gives an example from
a Hittite treaty of a stipulation in apodictic form (p. 7;
cp. p. 5 above); while, in regard to the latter, he argues
that it ". . . is hard to conceive of a lawcode which could
be more at variance from what we know of Canaanite culture,
than the Covenant Code" (p. 13). His own view is that, for
provenance, one need look no further than the Hittite covenants, whose stipulations ". . . are precisely a mixture of
case law and apodictic law very similar to the mixture found
in the so-called 'Covenant Code' of Exodus 21-23" (p. 7;

---

[1]Delbert R. Hillers, Covenant: The History of a
Biblical Idea (Baltimore: The Johns Hopkins Press, 1969),
pp. 89-92, illustrates the concreteness of the Covenant
Code in comparison with the Decalogue by placing below
several of the commandments of the Decalogue corresponding
laws from the Covenant Code. Some of these laws are in
apodictic and some in casuistic form. Our example, which
appears in his list, was previously noted by Mendenhall
(p. 16, fn. 38).

cp. p. 14).

The relevance of the Hittite treaty-form for an understanding of biblical law is worked out in detail in
Mendenhall's second section (pp. 24-50). After pointing
out that Hittite covenants may be divided into two types
--suzerainty treaties and parity treaties (p. 29)--he goes
on to delineate the covenant form as found in the Hittite
texts (pp. 31-35). "Nearly always," the following elements
are present:

1. The preamble. "This identifies the author of the covenant, giving his titles and attributes . . ." (p. 32).

2. The historical prologue describes the previous relations between the parties, with a special emphasis upon the
benevolent deeds of the suzerain on behalf of the vassal
(p. 32).

3. The stipulations state the obligations imposed by the
sovereign and accepted by the vassal. Among these are "the
prohibition of other foreign relationships outside the
Hittite Empire" and an annual appearance of the vassal before
the Hittite king (p. 33).

4. The deposit and public reading. The treaty document was
deposited in the sanctuary of the vassal for reading to the
public at stipulated intervals (p. 34).

5. The list of witnesses. The gods of both states are
listed as guarantors of the covenant, along with natural

35

elements; e.g., mountains, rivers, etc. (p. 34).

6. __Blessings__ __and__ __curses__. Things to be effected by the gods for obedience to, or breach of, the covenant (p. 34). The treaty, the written text of which contained these formal features, would have been ratified by a ". . . formal oath by which the vassal pledged his obedience" (p. 34).

Having established the covenant form, Mendenhall turns to an examination of the ". . . only two traditions . . . which fall into (that) form . . ." (p. 36): the Decalogue and the material embedded in the narrative of Josh. 24 (pp. 36-44). Here he discusses both the presence and __absence__ of the features of the covenant form in the two traditions. Though the Decalogue lacks the last three elements of the covenant form, these are to be found else-where in Israel's traditions (pp. 39-40). He concludes that, in early Israel, historical traditions "crystallized" about the covenant form, and stresses ". . . the fact that what we now call 'history' and 'law' (cp. the historical prologue and stipulations of the Hittite covenants) were bound up into an organic unit from the very beginnings of Israel itself" (p. 44).[1]

---

[1]In the teeth of, e.g., Gerhard von Rad, "The Form-Critical Problem of the Hexateuch," in __The__ __Problem__ __of__ __the__ __Hexateuch__ __and__ __Other__ __Essays__, trans. by E. W. Trueman Dicken (Edinburgh and London: Oliver & Boyd, 1965), pp. 1-78.

Finally, Mendenhall explains the prophetic reticence in speaking of the covenant, though the messages of the prophets ". . . are in the nature of an indictment for breach of covenant . . ." (p. 46). By the time of the prophets, another covenant tradition--the Davidic covenant--had become normative. Since the Davidic covenant ". . . guaranteed the continuation of the monarchy . . ." (and the state as well), for the prophets ". . . to maintain that Yahweh would destroy the nation, would be to attribute to Him breach of covenant" (p. 46). Thus the prophets ignored the Mosaic covenant and conveyed their message by the use of other figures.[1]

Mendenhall's study has received cogent criticism from Dennis McCarthy in the latter's doctoral dissertation, Treaty and Covenant.[2] In his introduction, McCarthy refers to Mendenhall's study and faults Mendenhall for a priori argumentation with respect to the covenant form (pp. 5-6). Mendenhall's argument proceeded: 1) there was a Sinai covenant; 2) the Hittite treaties exhibit the covenant form;

---

[1]A few of these "other figures" are indicated by Mendenhall on pp. 46-47. For the way in which the Bible resolves the conflict between the two covenant traditions, see David Noel Freedman, "Divine Commitment and Human Obligation," Interpretation, XVIII (1964), pp. 419-31.

[2]Dennis J. McCarthy, Treaty and Covenant (Rome: Pontifical Biblical Institute, 1963). The pages in parentheses from here through the first full paragraph on p. 40 refer to McCarthy's work.

3) the original form of the Sinai covenant was that of the
Hittite treaties. McCarthy says yes to 1, but no to 2 and
3. Concerning the second point, McCarthy argues that ". . .
there was more than one form of covenant" (p. 5). The
Hittite treaties were "contractual" covenants, based on oath,
". . . but the ancients knew of many another kind of cove-
nant-making technique" (p. 5). The chickens come home to
roost for Mendenhall when he moves from this assumption of
the covenant form to discuss the form of the Decalogue:

> This discussion sets out from the idea that the Dec-
> alogue is in the covenant form and so exerts itself
> to explain how so much of the form--witnesses, curses
> and blessings, oath--can have been omitted from the
> text.[1]

After an examination of the extra-biblical treaty
texts (pp. 15-106), McCarthy turns to the Old Testament
materials. He finds that the "central discourse" in
Deuteronomy (4:44-28:68) exhibits the treaty form (pp.
109-30), and that this form has influenced other material;
e.g., the Deuteronomic framework (pp. 131-40), I Sam. 12
(pp. 141-45), and Joshua 24 (pp. 145-51). With Sinai, however, it is a different story.

This is demonstrable, according to McCarthy, especially
after completing the literary-critical task of excising from
the Sinai narrative the Covenant Code with the promises which

---

[1]Ibid., p. 6.

were attached thereto and the historical material of 19:3b-8
(pp. 154-57).[1] When this is done, the narrative lacks a
curse or blessing formula, an element indispensable to the
treaty form (pp. 154-55). Even the material left to the
Sinai narrative creates serious misgivings. The introduction
(what remains of Ex. 19 and 20:2; though the latter may also
be secondary) is oriented, not toward what Yahweh has done in
the past, but toward his aweful presence (pp. 157-58)--the
theophany--and the definition of his person (p. 160).[2]
Further, the stipulations of the Hittite treaties are not
really comparable to the commandments of the Decalogue: the
former do not cover as wide a range of topics, lack the
terseness of the Decalogue's commands, and ". . . do not
really constitute anything like the litany-like sequence of
'thou shalt nots'" which are characteristic of the Decalogue
(pp. 159-60). Finally, Ex. 24 shows that the alliance was
ratified by rites, rather than by oath (pp. 161-63). Thus,
the original sequence of the Sinai narrative was: "coming

---

[1]Even were these pericopae to be retained, the case for
Ex. 19-24 as exhibiting the treaty form would not be advanced, for the promises of 23:20 ff. are not "well adapted
to the function of covenant blessings" (p. 154), and the
history in Ex. 19 is not a true historical prologue (p. 155).

[2]The argument against Ex. 20:2 as an historical prologue is buoyed by a grammatical observation: in an historical prologue, the "suzerain . . . speaks . . . in the
third person"; while, in Ex. 20:2, Yahweh speaks ". . . in
the first person" (p. 160).

of Yahwe, proclamation of His will, and rites by which the alliance was ratified" (p. 162), a sequence which ". . . reveals an idea of covenant . . . in which the ritual looms larger than the verbal and contractual" (p. 163). The Sinai narrative, then, does not exhibit the treaty form. This is true of both the E and J elements of the story (pp. 163-67).

McCarthy concludes that Israel's covenant with Yahweh is conceived of in two ways: "The older, that of Sinai, is ritual, the second uses the contractual treaty form" (p. 173). The later tradition ". . . reaches its flowering in Dt." (p. 174), but, even there, does not completely displace the older view--rather, it simply incorporates it (p. 173).

How does the foregoing discussion bear upon our own concern? Both Mendenhall and McCarthy would agree that law appears in the Pentateuch in a covenant context. They disagree in respect to the Sinai narrative: i.e., is the law (Decalogue) to be understood as the stipulations of a sovereign whose beneficence has been revealed in history, and to whom the people are bound by oath (treaty context) or, is it to be understood as the revealed will of one who appeared in a theophany, and to whom they are allied by rites (ritual context)? The studies of Westermann and Bach (cp. pp. 26-29 and 30-32, above) have noted the affinity of prophetic accusation (i.e., the Ac. portion of the PJS) to apodictic law. We are now led to wonder whether the Prophetic Judgment-

Speeches indicate the context in which this law was understood. Was it a covenant context? And, if so, do the
speeches imply (or, are we able to infer) the form which the
covenant assumed?

Leaving the Mendenhall-McCarthy debate to focus on
the earlier part of Mendenhall's study, we are led to
another observation regarding the place of the PJS (cp. pp.
13-15, above). To state the matter using Mendenhall's terms:
the PJS presupposes a situation where legal sanctions and
legal techniques have failed. Normally, according to the
concept of corporate personality, the deity will punish the
community for the offense of any of its members (pp. 4-5).
However, this can be averted by legal action (p. 5) --by
putting the offender to death, or by asserting that a
particular act is not, in fact, contrary to legal policy.
(Ex. 22:1-2, a law in casuistic form is an example of the
latter. It states that, under certain circumstances, the
killing of a thief is not murder.) Now, what the PJS says
is that an offense has been committed, and that the deity
will punish. This can only mean that the community has mis-
used or disused the means which it has available for protecting it from divine punishment.

Finally, the viewing of law in the context of covenant
invites another question. If there is a covenant, who are
the parties involved? One party, of course, is God. The

other, equally clearly, is Israel. However, is it possible
to define more precisely this Israel who is bound, by covenant, to obey the law?

Martin Noth, "The Laws in the Pentateuch: Their Assumptions
and Meaning," <u>The Laws in the Pentateuch and Other Studies</u>,
trans. by D. R. Ap-Thomas (Edinburgh and London: Oliver &
Boyd, 1966), pp. 1-107.

    Only the first two sections of Noth's essay (pp. 1-60)
which carry the discussion down to the Exile are of concern
to us. Noth doubts the propriety of speaking of "the law"
in the Old Testament, since what we find is "a series of
different <u>literary units</u>" in which "'law' is present" (p. 6).
These originally independent units contain material of
diverse form (casuistic and apodictic) and content (social
and cultic regulations), and "very different dates . . .
must be assigned to . . ." them (pp. 7-8). Only the common
attribution of these elements to Moses and their insertion
". . . for the most part into the narrative tradition about
the sojourn of the Israelite tribes at Sinai . . ." which
gives them a literary proximity suggest a "superficial"
unity (p. 9). Nevertheless, one finds the same precepts in
different literary units and there is a continuity of themes
from the earliest to the latest legislation (p. 9), so that
"within the Old Testament as a whole the 'law' . . . appears
as an entity . . . and can and must be treated as one"
(p. 10). Noth's immediate interest is in the presuppositions
for the existence of the Old Testament laws: i.e.. in the

42

historical framework in which they originated (pp. 10-11).

In light of what is known of other law-codes, one possibility is that Israel's laws were state laws (p. 12). The difficulty with this view is that ". . . the Old Testament law-codes have not been satisfactorily expounded as state laws" (p. 14). They ". . . do not presuppose monarchy, or any particular form of government, as a necessary state of affairs" (p. 18).

What these laws do presuppose is a community which has the following features: 1) a "common link with Yahweh (which) was constitutive for the community" (p. 20); 2) "separation from those inhabitants of Palestine (i.e., the Canaanites) who had no part in this association" (p. 21); 3) a conquest tradition which ". . . knows of a previous sojourn of the Israelite tribes in Egypt and their release from that land" (p. 23); and 4) a "name of high antiquity --the name 'Israel'" (p. 25).[1] Just such a community was "the sacral confederacy of the twelve tribes of Israel," which came into existence "between the occupation of Palestine . . . and the first attempt to form a state under Saul

---

[1]Noth indicates which law codes ascribe which features to the community presupposed by it (pp. 20-28); e.g.: "Particularly in Deuteronomy and the Holiness Code the community addressed in the laws is emphatically distinguished from the 'Canaanites,' who are tied to 'other gods'" (p. 22).

. . ." (p. 28) and continued as a living reality throughout
the monarchial period until the events of the beginning of
the sixth century brought about its dissolution (pp. 60-61).[1]
This community was linked to Yahweh by a common cult with the
ark as its visible center (p. 29). It bore the name Israel
(p. 32), and its existence as a tangible entity during the
monarchial period is attested by the use of the name Israel
with a religious reference at a time when the term also had
a precise political meaning (p. 33).

What provides the link between the entities "Yahweh,"
"Israel," and "laws"? i.e., what is the framework which
validates the laws? The Sinai tradition of a covenant between Yahweh and Israel (p. 37). The Old Testament clearly
associates covenant and law, and it is the ". . . situation
established by means of the 'covenant' . . ." (whose "fixed
form" was the sacral confederacy) within which the laws
apply (p. 41).

In light of Noth's insistence that the law-codes of
the Old Testament are not to be understood as state law,
how ". . . are we to envisage the role of the deuteronomic
law . . . under King Josiah" (p. 41)? Deuteronomy was not
intended as state legislation (p. 43). Through Josiah's
agency a covenant between God and people was concluded (which

---

[1]For substantiation, Noth refers the reader to his Das
System der zwölf Stämme Israels.

44

"was simply a renewal or reconfirmation of the Sinai covenant . . .") by means of a sacral ceremony (not an act of
state), which made Deuteronomy operative (p. 45). That
Josiah should have taken the initiative may be attributed to
his position as the leader of the "qehal Yahweh" (p. 46).
However, when Josiah, as <u>King</u>, began to implement some of
the Deuteronomic requirements, it became the ultimate fate
of the deuteronomic code that it be <u>treated</u> as state law
(pp. 47-48).

In the final pages of his discussion of the situation
in the pre-Exilic period, Noth buttresses his thesis that
the Old Testament laws are not to be understood as state law
by reference to the content of the laws. Peculiar to the
Old Testament codes (as opposed to their ancient Near
Eastern counterparts) are "provisions which seek to ensure
the exclusive nature of the relationship between God and
people . . ." (p. 51).[1] These would be of little relevance
for ". . . areas with a completely 'Canaanite' population,
. . ." and could hardly ". . . have been intended as state
law" (p. 60).

That part of Noth's thesis which is of interest to

---

[1]For example, Noth understands the purpose of the
deuteronomic requirement of the unity of cult places (p. 52)
and the regulations about clean and unclean animals (pp. 56-
59) to be the protection of the community from the influence
of foreign cults.

us contains three <u>separable</u> elements:

1. That the Pentateuchal legislation presupposes a community which is characterized by certain features.

2. That this legislation (in whole or in part) was never <u>intended</u> to be state legislation; though, in fact, Deuteronomy was mistakenly treated as such.

3. That the community presupposed by the laws was a <u>living entity</u> from the period of the Judges to the Exile. This community was a "sacral confederacy," and was comparable to the ancient Greek amphictyonies.

It is the third point which has occasioned the most controversy, though not in connection with the work under discussion, but with Noth's theory of an Israelite amphictyony as set forth in his <u>Das System der zwölf Stämme Israels</u> (Stuttgart: W. Kohlhammer, 1930). A fresh look at Noth's <u>System</u> has recently been taken by G. W. Anderson, "Israel: Amphictyony: ʿAm; Ḳāhāl; ʿEdāh," <u>Translating & Understanding the Old Testament</u>, ed. by Harry Thomas Frank and William L. Reed (Nashville and New York: Abingdon Press, 1970), pp. 135-51. Anderson's view is that while ". . . Noth did indeed adduce good grounds for the view that a twelve-tribe system existed in the premonarchic period . . . there appears to be little evidence of the distinctive features of an amphictyony" (pp. 148-49). Telling against an amphictyony is the evidence from the period of the Judges that the

Israelite tribes lacked centralization and the absence of
anything ". . . substantial concerning a central sanctuary
or a succession of sanctuaries" (p. 149). According to
Anderson, however, this does not preclude an Israelite unity,
a unity which preceded the settlement and proceeded from the
". . . establishment of the Sinai covenant between Yahweh
and the Israelite tribes" (p. 149). In this view, Josh. 24
records not the establishment of an amphictyony, but the
admission to the Sinai covenant ". . . after the invasion,
of diverse elements, tribal and other" (p. 150).

It seems to us that Noth presents us with a not alto-
gether satisfactory either-or: either the laws envisage a
"grouping in Israelite history" (since the state is out, the
only candidate is the "sacral confederacy" modelled on the
Greek amphictyonic pattern), or "a purely imaginary situation" (p. 28). The weakness of Noth's view is that, for
him, identity (a "people") seems to imply a _political_
entity.[1] And, if there is any place in history where this
assumption is belied, it is precisely the story of the people
"Israel."

We agree with Noth that the Pentateuchal legislation
addresses a community which has as its characteristic

---

[1]This is also the gist of Bright's criticism of Noth's
History of Israel. See John Bright, _Early Israel in Recent_
History Writing (London: SCM Press, 1960), pp. 83-85, 111-
126, _passim_.

features those delineated by Noth. We agree, further, that
this community was a living reality (though at some times
more "alive" than at others). We do not agree that the community in an amphictyonic form is a necessary presupposition
of the laws. A people defined by a covenant relationship is
sufficient.

Noth provides us with a viable procedure. He looks to
the Pentateuchal legislation in its context to provide the
clues to the identity of the people for whom it is the law.
For this way of working--from law(s) to people--we are
grateful to him.

We must now speak more precisely of the nature and
course of our investigation.

We call the first part of our study "The Law in the
Prophets"; a title which at once describes the territory
and the quest. Our focus in this section will be upon the
PJS and its variants from the earliest examples to the Exile.
The terrain has been explored and its boundaries fixed by
Westermann, and he will serve as our Baedeker. We shall pay
special attention to the speeches commonly ascribed to Amos,
Micah, Isaiah of Jerusalem, and Jeremiah. This limitation
frees us from the necessity of attending to the multiplicity
of critical problems which an examination of all the pre-
exilic prophets would require, yet retains for our discussion
material of sufficient quantity and temporal breadth.

We shall begin by showing that prophetic accusation presupposes a standard to which those whom the prophets accuse are bound. A comparison of the content of some prophetic accusations (it is in the Ac. portion of the PJS that prophetic accusation is found) with certain Pentateuchal laws will suggest that a variety of laws often comprised this standard. It is the sum of these laws which are inferred from a comparison of the content of prophetic accusation with the Pentateuchal legislation that we call "The Law in the Prophets." The Pentateuchal legislation is a necessary control, because prophets accuse people of things other than breach of legal injunctions (e.g., of attempting to silence a prophet; cp. Westermann, pp. 105-06), and it is only by reference to the Pentateuchal legislation that we can tell that a law is involved.

The object of our quest will be to describe this "law" which underlies prophetic accusation. The greater part of our first chapter will be devoted to seeing whether the Pentateuchal form of those laws whose content is paralleled in prophetic accusations is always apodictic, or whether there will be a similarity in content to laws in casuistic form as well. Our reading of Westermann suggests—a suggestion which Bach's study reinforces—the possibility that the Pentateuchal laws will all conform to one or another of Alt's apodictic categories.

We shall see that the prophets seem to assume that the laws which underlie their accusations are binding on those whom they accuse. In our second chapter, we shall attempt to elicit from the Judgment-Speeches of our four prophets the grounds on which they understand the "law" to be authoritative. Mendenhall's work, pointing to a connection between law and covenant, will here give impetus to our investigation.

In the third chapter, we shall ask the question of "The Law in the Prophets" which Noth asked of the Pentateuchal legislation: "Who is addressed in these laws?" With the answer to this question, our first section will come to an end.

Having gained a picture of "The Law in the Prophets," in the beginning of the second part of our study we will shift our focus to the Pentateuch to observe in a different context the laws which underlie our prophets' accusations.[1] Here they will be found alongside other laws which are of no apparent concern to our prophets. We shall see how the Pentateuch attaches varying degrees of importance to the laws it contains, and that it envisages a variety of ways of dealing with those who transgress these laws.

When our Pentateuchal sojourn is finished, we shall

---

[1]When we speak of "our prophets" we mean Amos, Micah, Isaiah of Jerusalem, and Jeremiah.

return to our prophets--better placed to understand the
relationship of the prophets to the law. In the PJS, the
law and the prophets come together, and from this union
stems revelation: the communication of the way and will
of God.

PART I.   THE LAW IN THE PROPHETS

I.   THE NATURE OF THE LAW IN THE PROPHETS

Reflections on an Incident in the Life
of Jeremiah lead to some Questions

Deeply ingrained within the individual and the human
community is this almost insuperable barrier to communication: an auditor hears what he wishes to hear--he becomes
bothered about what he wants to become bothered about. This
recurrent bane of the interlocutor's existence is evidenced
again and again in the lives of the prophets. Jeremiah 26,
the narrative account of the prophet's trial for treason, is
a typical example. First, the report of what the prophet
said:

> Thus says the Lord: if you will not listen to me by
> walking in my law which I have set before you, by lis-
> tening to the words of my servants the prophets whom
> I continued to send to you with urgency, though you
> did not heed, then I will make this house like Shiloh,
> and this city a curse for all the nations of the earth.
> (26:4-6)

The narrator records the auditors' response:

> Why did you prophesy in the name of the Lord: "This
> house will be like Shiloh, this city an uninhabited
> ruin" (26:9)?

It was the Shiloh bit which the people heard--which they
could not stomach.

Later, Jeremiah was to experience a similar reaction, this time to the written word. The reactor, on this occasion, was not the people, but king Jehoiakim. Jeremiah, now in hiding,[1] had had Baruch, his amanuensis, write on a scroll what God had bidden Jeremiah:[2]

> . . . all the words which I have spoken to you concerning Jerusalem,[3] Judah, and all the nations, from the time I spoke to you in the days of Josiah to this very day (36:2).

This scroll was eventually read before the king and consigned to the flames; whereupon Jeremiah was then commanded to:

> Take another scroll and write on it all the former words which were on the first scroll, which Jehoiakim the king of Judah burned (36:28).

Further, Jeremiah was to include a personal word to the king:

> To Jehoiakim king of Judah you shall say, "Thus says the Lord, you, yourself, have burned this scroll, with the words, 'Why did you write on it that the king of

---

[1]See Sheldon H. Blank, _Jeremiah: Man and Prophet_ (Cincinnati: Hebrew Union College Press, 1961), p. 27, for his translation of עצור in Jeremiah 36:5 as "in hiding."

[2]For discussions of the content of the original scroll, see Otto Eissfeldt, _The Old Testament: An Introduction_, trans. by Peter R. Ackroyd (New York and Evanston: Harper & Row, 1965), pp. 350-54 and Georg Fohrer, _Introduction to the Old Testament_, trans. by David E. Green (Nashville and New York: Abingdon Press, 1968), pp. 392-94. We agree with Fohrer both as to the hopelessness in attempting to reconstruct the original scroll and as to the fact that it would have contained invective as well as threat.

[3]Following LXX.

Babylon will surely come to devastate this land, and
to cut off from it man and beast?'" (36:29)

Of all the words of the first scroll, it was the announcement of the imminent destruction of the land which most
angered the king--which he truly heard.

Yet, by this time, Jeremiah should not have been
surprised at what people hear, what they remember, that to
which they react with anger. At Jeremiah's trial, and on
his behalf, the words of a prophetic predecessor are recalled:

> Micah the Morashtite prophesied in the days of Heze-
> kiah king of Judah, and said to all the people of Ju-
> dah: "Zion will be ploughed as a field, Jerusalem
> will be a heap of ruins and the temple mount forested
> high places" (26:18).

Fortunately, we have in the book of Micah the pericope which
these words conclude.[1] It contains an indictment of Zion's
leaders, for which the destruction of Zion is announced as
punishment. That is, it is Micah's announcement of disaster
which is recalled by the elders as words worthy of the prophet's dispatch.[2] It is apparent from these examples that what

---

[1]Mic. 3:9-12.

[2]Klaus Koch (Biblical Tradition, p. 212) accounts for
the elders' quotation of only the final portion of Micah's
prophecy on the ground that the prediction of disaster (as
opposed to the "diatribe") "always comprises the real substance of the prophecy." It seems to me, however, that one
might plausibly argue that the reason that only these of
Micah's words were recalled was that they, alone, were
germane to Jeremiah's case: both men had prophesied the
destruction of temple and city; Micah was not put to death:

upset a prophet's auditors, that which they truly heard, was
the announcement of disaster.

Yet, what interests us is not what the people got upset
about, nor even why they got upset about it; but, what they
didn't get upset about, and why they didn't get upset about
it. For this, we must turn to the text of Jeremiah's "temple
sermon"; the address which had occasioned his trial.[1] It is
a perfect homily; easily divisible into three parts. It
begins with a plea:

> Thus says the Lord of hosts, the God of Israel, amend
> your ways and your deeds, that I may let you dwell in
> this place. Do not trust in deceptive words, "The
> temple of the Lord, the temple of the Lord, the temple
> of the Lord are these."[2] Rather, if you really amend
> your ways and your deeds, really execute justice be-
> tween men, and neither oppress sojourner, orphan, or
> widow nor shed innocent blood in this place, and don't
> follow other gods to your own detriment; then, I will
> let you dwell in this place, in the land which I gave

---

therefore, Jeremiah should not be put to death. Either way,
it is clear that what provokes antipathy to the prophet is
the announcement of disaster.

[1]That 26:3-6 is a summary of the "temple sermon,"
which is found in more complete form in 7:2-15, is so generally accepted that it does not need demonstration. Cp.
John Bright, _Jeremiah_ (vol. 21 of _The Anchor Bible_, Garden
City: Doubleday & Company, 1965), p. 171.

[2]For his Jeremiah class, Sheldon Blank explained the
plural, "these," as follows: "The words were doubtless
accompanied by a sweeping gesture to include the various
parts of the temple complex." The "deceptive words," which
Jeremiah quotes, may well have been spoken originally by
pseudo-prophets for whom, as A. S. van der Woude has shown
in "Micah in Dispute with the Pseudo-Prophets," _VT_, XIX
(April, 1969), p. 257, "Zion-theology was a decisive factor
in their lives and thoughts."

to your fathers . . . (7:3-7).

Plea gives way to accusation:

> Look (as a matter of fact), you do trust in deceptive
> words to no avail. Can you steal, murder, commit
> adultery, swear falsely, burn incense to Baal, follow
> other gods whom you have not known, and (still) come
> and stand in my presence in this house . . . and say,
> "We are safe"? . . . (7:8-10).

And, a summary of the accusation:[1]

> Because you have done all these things, it is the Lord
> speaking, and though I spoke to you persistently you
> did not listen, and though I called you, you did not
> answer . . . (7:13).

leads to the announcement of disaster:

> Therefore I will do to this house . . . in which you
> trust . . . as I did to Shilo (7:14).

Let us speak of parents and children. When a parent
encounters a disobedient child, he reprimands and punishes
him. To the parental reprimand and announced punishment the
child will normally react in one of the following ways.

1. He will admit guilt and accept the punishment. This
almost never happens (at least I never did, and my own
children don't).

2. He will deny guilt. This denial takes one of two forms:
either, "I didn't do it"; or, "I did it, but . . . (the child
goes on to plead extenuating circumstances)."

3. He will argue about the propriety of the punishment.

---

[1]So Westermann, Grundformen, pp. 130 and 149 (fn.
28). Westermann attributes the "Zusammenfassung" to the
Deuteronomists.

4. He will cry: either because, recognizing his guilt, he hopes to forestall punishment by playing upon the executioner's sympathy; or, because he experiences the pain of the punishment in anticipation of it.

5. He will vent his wrath on the accuser, hoping to forestall punishment thereby.

If one may equate those who heard Jeremiah's sermon with children, it is clear that the auditors chose a form of the fifth alternative; they tried to forestall the announced disaster by attacking its source.[1] What interests us is that they did not attempt the second alternative--they did not try to refute the accusation. Why did they not seek to deny their guilt? Is it not strange that prophets go around making accusations and announcing disaster while the object of such denunciation, be it an individual or a group, does not attempt to deny guilt? We venture to suggest two reasons to account for this behaviour; the first as an

---

[1] They think that by putting the speaker to death they will render the words ineffective. However, it is the point of Jeremiah's defense that by his removal nothing will be accomplished, for the real author of the words is not Jeremiah, but God. That this is indeed Jeremiah's argument has been ably demonstrated by Blank in Jeremiah, pp. 18-20. Blank has also shown (Ibid., p. 29) that the notion that words are made ineffective by destroying their source stands behind the incident related in chapter 36. Since the scroll is being destroyed (vs. 23), there is no longer any need for fear (cp. vs. 16 with vs. 24). The method is consistent: if the announced disaster is written, one gets rid of the scroll; if it is spoken, one gets rid of the speaker.

explanation of the focus on the attempt to forestall disaster, the second as an explanation of the lack of an attempt
to deny guilt.

1. "Sticks and stones may break my bones, but names can
never hurt me." As Westermann has shown: in the simplest
form of the PJS it is the AD which, alone, is the real word
of God; being designated as such by the MF plus "therefore."[1]
Being the word of God--so immediate, powerful, effective--the
attempt to render it ineffective must receive first priority.[2] The AD, being God's word, is so threatening that
the Ac. on which it is grounded pales into insignificance.

2. The nature of the PJS is such that it does not brook
denial of guilt; for its raison d'être is that a transgression has, in fact, taken place. The point is Westermann's:

> Voraussetzung des Ergehens eines GE (Gerichtswort an
> Einzelne) ist ein Vergehen dessen, an den das Wort
> gerichtet ist . . .[3]

That is to say, that portion of the PJS which we have referred to as the Ac. borders on being an assertion of guilt.

---

[1]Grundformen, p. 94. We have quoted the passage from
Westermann on p. 8, above. For the abbreviations used
throughout this paper to designate the Prophetic Judgment-
Speech and its parts, see p. vii.

[2]Isaiah 55:10-11 and the Balaam oracle of Num 23:19
forcefully express the idea of the effective power of the
Word. In fn. 1, page 58, above, we discuss two attempts to
render it ineffective.

[3]Grundformen, p. 94. We would declare the same
"Voraussetzung" for the "Gerichtsankündigung gegen Israel."

This, in turn, properly demands a framework within which guilt can be ascertained; a standard to which the accused is committed and by which he can be judged; a common ground for accused and accuser which can obviate any plea of extenuating circumstances.[1]

Such a standard, in turn, evokes certain questions:

What is it?
On what ground is it binding?
Who is bound?

Since a variety of laws will be seen to comprise this standard, and since the standard will be elicited from prophetic speeches and primarily from those contained in that canonical unit which is designated "the prophets," we call our consideration of these questions: "The Law in the Prophets."

The Nature of the Law in the Prophets

We begin our investigation with an examination of the content of Jeremiah's accusation in the "temple sermon."

Can you steal, murder, commit adultery, swear falsely,
burn incense to Baal, follow other gods whom you have

---

[1]Walter Beyerlin, in Die Kulttraditionen Israels in der Verkündigung des Propheten Micha (Göttingen: Vandenhoeck & Ruprecht, 1959), pp. 42-64, passim, also sees a previously existing standard as a logical necessity. He defines this standard as the amphictyonic law, made known to the people through the cult. However, he posits it in relation to the AD; while, for us, it is the logical antecedent of the Ac. Beyerlin's statement is: "Nur die bei den Hörern der prophetischen Botschaft schon vorhandene Kenntnis von Jahwes Recht und Gerechtigkeit kann Anknüpfungspunkt und Schlüssel zur Deutung des angekündigten Unheils sein" (p. 50).

not known . . . (7:9).

Yes, the words have a familiar ring! Jeremiah

   . . . knew of "the ten commandments." . . . in effect
he was asking: How many of the "ten commandments"
would you defy--and with presumed impunity?[1]

---

[1]Blank, <u>Jeremiah</u>, p. 14. While Jer. 7:9 raises a
number of questions, we shall direct our attention to but
two.
1. To which commandment does השבע לשקר refer? Blank (p. 14)
and Bright (<u>Jeremiah</u>, p. 56) refer it to "You shall not bear
false witness against your neighbor." Eduard Nielsen (<u>Ten
Commandments</u>, p. 112) apparently refers it to his third
commandment (See p. 84 for his attempt to reproduce the
original form of the Decalogue and p. 87 for his understanding of the meaning of "Thou shalt not take the name of
Yahweh in vain."). Paul Volz in <u>Der Prophet Jeremia</u> (2d ed.;
Leipzig: A. Deichertsche Verlagsbuchhandlung, 1928), p. 91,
gives us our choice; while Anthony Phillips in <u>Ancient
Israel's Criminal Law</u> (Oxford: Basil Blackwell, 1970),
p. 148, rejects the position of Blank and Bright and makes
reference to "Thou shalt have no other gods before me."
Closer in linguistic proximity to Jeremiah's accusation than
any of the Decalogue commandments is Lev. 19:12a, and closer
still is the form which Gerhard von Rad, in <u>Studies in
Deuteronomy</u> (London: SCM, 1953), p. 28, suggests lies behind it: לא תשבע לשקר. The linguistic affinity to Lev. 19:
12a, together with the strange order of Jeremiah's accusations (as opposed to the traditional Decalogue order),
suggests to me that we should not be thinking of any particular formulation of the Decalogue as standing behind Jeremiah's accusations, but simply of "traditional law." Further, I plead ignorant with regard to what Jeremiah is
accusing his hearers of when he says השבע לשקר; I only know
that he knew, and they knew.
2. If, however, השבע לשקר really does refer to "You shall
not bear false witness against your neighbor"; then, one may
ask whether Jeremiah has in mind the text of Exodus or
Deuteronomy. Blank (p. 14) opts for Deuteronomy. Here,
however, one is faced with Deuteronomy's עד שוא as opposed
to עד שקר in Exodus. It is possible, however, that in Deuteronomy, as well as Exodus, the original word was שקר. It
was changed only later, under the influence of שוא in
Deut. 5:11 (cp. Nielsen, <u>Ten Commandments</u>, p. 42). In any
case, the answers to these questions are not crucial for us;
we are only interested in the general correspondence of

It is, then, the people's transgression of a number of
the ten commandments which forms the basis for Jeremiah's
accusation, consequent upon which will be the disaster which
Jeremiah announces and which draws the people's ire. Moreover, this was not the only occasion on which transgression
of the ten commandments formed the content of prophetic
accusation:

> Uriah the Hittite you have smitten with the sword, and
> his wife you have taken for your own wife.
> (II Sam. 12:9b)

But, is it only transgression of the ten commandments
which draws a prophetic tirade? To king Jehoiakim Jeremiah
said:

> Woe to the one who builds his house by unrighteousness
> and his upper chambers by injustice; who makes his
> neighbor work for him for nothing, not paying him his
> wages (22:13).[1]

Such behavior is clearly prohibited:

> Do not oppress your neighbor or rob him. Let not the
> wages of a hired man remain with you overnight until
> morning (Lev. 19:13).

> Do not oppress a poor and needy hired man . . . On the
> day he works you shall pay his hire before sunset.
> (Deut. 24: 14-15)

While, in content, a Decalogue prohibition does not parallel

Jeremiah's accusations to the prohibitions now contained in
the Decalogue.

[1]The prophet here uses a "Woe-Speech" rather than a
PJS as the vehicle for his accusation. For the "Woe-Speech"
as a variant of the PJS see Westermann, Grundformen, pp.
136-40.

this accusation; in form, the prohibitions to which it is
related belong, with those of the Decalogue, to those groups
of laws which Albrecht Alt has given the designation "apodictic."[1] That non-Decalogue, apodictic law can form the
ground of an accusation leading to punishment, poor Naboth
learned:[2]

> Two base fellows came and sat opposite him, and the base
> fellows gave testimony against Naboth in the presence of
> the people: "Naboth has cursed God and the king" (I
> Kings 21:13).

> God you shall not revile, nor shall you curse a leader
> of your people (Ex. 22:27).

That among the pre-literary prophets Jeremiah had predecessors whose accusations were grounded in apodictic, non-
Decalogue law is at least possible;[3] that in Amos, he

---

[1]For the terms "apodictic" and "casuistic" law, and a
brief summary of Alt's characterization of each, see pp.
2-3, above. Alt's distinction is useful to us in that what
we notice is that the content of prophetic accusation corresponds to the content of those laws which he has designated
"apodictic."

[2]Westermann (Grundformen, p. 105) emphasizes the formal
similarity of the accusation (I Kings 21:13) to the prohibition (Ex. 22:27). If one reads אלהים for להם (a tiqqun
sopherim) in I Sam. 3:13; then, the transgression of the sons
of Eli is also to be related to Ex. 22:27. Phillips
(Criminal Law, pp. 41-42) points out that a transgression of
Ex. 22:27 "need not be confined to spoken actions" (p. 41).

[3]Westermann (Grundformen, p. 95) relates the transgression of Ahab (I Kings 21) to Ex. 21:12, and that of
Ahaziah (II Kings 1) to Ex. 23:13. Murray Newman, "The
Prophetic Call of Samuel," Israel's Prophetic Heritage, ed.
by Bernhard W. Anderson and Walter Harrelson (New York:
Harper & Brothers, 1962), p. 95, sees Ahab as having violated
"the Mosaic prohibitions of murder and theft." It is in

certainly did, has been demonstrated in an article to which
we have already had occasion to refer, Robert Bach's "Gottesrecht und weltliches Recht in der Verkündigung des Propheten Amos."[1]

After examining the "reproaches" in Amos, Bach arrives
at the following conclusion:

> Amos greift in den Begründungen seiner Unheils-
> ankündigungen nicht auf beide Zweige des israelitischen
> Rechts (i.e., apodictic and casuistic law) zurück,
> sondern nur auf einen von ihnen, nämlich das
> apodiktische Recht.[2]

Newman's favor that the accusation (I Kings 21:19) uses the
word הרצחת (cp. Ex. 20:13), while the word in the apodictic
law in Ex. 21:12 is מכה . However, if a "Mosaic prohibition" also stands behind the charge of "taking possession,"
it is probably the prohibition of "coveting." For a discussion of the eighth and tenth commandments see J. J. Stamm,
The Ten Commandments in Recent Research, trans. with addi-
tions by M. E. Andrew (London: SCM Press, 1967), pp. 101-07.
Stamm shows that חמד ". . . does not only mean 'covet' as an
impulse of the will, but that it also includes the intrigues
which lead to the taking possession of that which was coveted"
(p. 103). If we may think of I Sam. 3:13 as having been
spoken, originally, by a prophet, then it was related to
apodictic, non-Decalogue law (see previous fn.).

[1]See above, pp. 30-31.

[2]Ibid., p. 33. Bach examines the "reproaches" (Bach's
"reproach" equals Westermann's Ac.) on pp. 25-33. Actually,
Bach's assertion is even stronger than what we have quoted
suggests, for he goes on: "Diese ausschliessliche Gebund-
enheit an das apodiktische Recht geht so weit, dass er sich
gelegentlich ausdrücklich gegen das kasuistische Recht wendet"
(p. 33. Evidence for this extreme statement is to be found
on p. 29.). R. E. Clements, Prophecy and Covenant (London:
SCM, 1965), p. 76, fn. 2, tries to refute Bach by suggesting
that Amos "points out breaches of case law." His refutation
is hardly successful, since Bach has already anticipated and
dismissed Clements' examples ("Gottesrecht," pp. 29, 31-33).

Later on, we shall be pointing out how the content of a
number of Amos' accusations corresponds to that of certain
apodictic laws;[1] now, we must stress the twofold value which
Bach's study has for us: first, along with Jer. 22:13, it
extends the basis of prophetic accusation beyond the Decalogue to the general category of apodictic law; and second,
it excludes casuistic law as a basis for such accusation.
While Bach makes this assertion of sole dependence on
apodictic law only for Amos, the question arises whether this
might be true of other prophets as well. Apropos of this is
Walter Beyerlin's monograph, Die Kulttraditionen Israels in
der Verkündigung des Propheten Micha.[2] While the demonstration of the dependence of Micah on apodictic law was not
Beyerlin's purpose, his examination of Micah's accusations
has constant reference to apodictic law and only to such
law.[3]

---

[1]Cp. pp. 107-09, below.

[2]Op. cit.

[3]It is Beyerlin's thesis that Micah's oracles presuppose amphictyonic law. He treats the legal background
on pp. 50-64. In only one case (2:8a/ to Ex. 22:25-26 and
Deut. 24:13, 17) does he refer an accusation of Micah to
casuistic-type law (pp. 60-61). Bach ("Gottesrecht," p. 29),
however, sees behind the "light casuistic style" of the present form of the Exodus and Deuteronomy passages an origin in
apodictic law. Martin Noth also claims that the casuistic
formulation of Ex. 22:25-26 is secondary in Exodus: A
Commentary, trans. by J. S. Bowden (London: SCM Press, 1962),
p. 186.

But if, as a result of these studies and our own brief
look at Jeremiah, we may say that apodictic law did form a
basis upon which a prophet might accuse his people and jus-
tify his AD, may we also say--as Bach does with regard to
Amos' accusations and as Beyerlin's study shows to have been
the case with Micah--that prophetic accusation is _never_
grounded in casuistic law? We can find but one passage where
a casuistic law is the apparent basis of a prophetic accusation:

> Thus says the Lord, the God of Israel: I made a cove-
> nant with your fathers when I brought them forth from
> the land of Egypt, from the house of bondage, with these
> words, "Every seven years[1] each of you must set free his
> fellow Hebrew who has sold himself to you and has served
> you six years . . ." But your fathers didn't obey
> me--they paid no attention. But you have just turned
> around and done what pleased me by proclaiming liberty,
> each to his neighbor, and made a covenant in my pres-
> ence . . . ; whereupon, you turned around again and
> profaned my name by taking back each of you his male and
> female slaves whom you had set free[2] and subjecting them
> again to slavery. Therefore, thus says the Lord: Since
> you did not obey me by proclaiming liberty each to his

---

[1]Bright, _Jeremiah_, p. 222 explains our translation:
"Every seven years. Literally 'at the end of seven years.'
But it is actually at the end of six years, as the verse
makes clear; the sense is, 'when the seventh year arrives.'
Nevertheless we should not emend to 'six' (so RSV following
LXX), for the language of the verse is drawn from Deut. 15:1,
12, where the same expression occurs." Phillips (_Criminal
Law_, pp. 76-7) takes the view that Jeremiah and Deuteronomy
mean what they say: "at the end of seven years"; in contra-
distinction to Exodus.

[2]I have omitted לנפשם in vs. 16. Bright (_Jeremiah_,
p. 222) and Wilhelm Rudolph in _Jeremia_ (Tübingen: J. C. B.
Mohr, 1947), p. 188, cp. with Deut. 21:14. Bright translates: "to go where they wished."

brother, and each to his neighbor; I am about to pro-
claim liberty to you--it is the Lord speaking--to sword,
to pestilence, and to famine . . . And I will make the
men who transgressed my covenant . . . which they made
in my presence like[1] the calf which they cut in two and
passed between its parts . . . ; that is, I will give
them into the power of their enemies . . . and their
corpses shall serve as food for the carrion birds and
wild beasts (Jeremiah 34:13-20).

It is the recollection of a commitment made by Israel

at the time of the Exodus that poses the problem:

Every seven years each of you must set free his fellow
Hebrew who has sold himself to you and has served you
six years (34:14).

Ex. 21:2-6 and Deut. 15:12-18 both record laws formulated in

casuistic style which provide for the release at the end of

six years of servitude of a Hebrew who has sold himself into

slavery for debt. The passage from Deuteronomy begins:

If (כי) your fellow Hebrew, man or woman, sells himself
to you, he shall serve you six years, and in the seventh
year you shall set him free.
(15:12)

That it is the Deuteronomic formulation of the law which the

Jeremiah passage has in mind is clear, both because of lan-

guage and because female slaves were included in the manu-

mission proclaimed by Zedekiah.[2]

---

[1]Following the suggestion of Rudolph in BH[3] and reading
כעגל for העגל in vs. 18.

[2]Bright (Jeremiah, p. 222) and Julius A. Bewer in The
Prophets (New York: Harper & Brothers, 1949), p. 268, make
the point that Jer. 34:13 quotes the Hebrew of Deut. 15:1, 12
(see p. 66, fn. 1, above). Deut. 15:1 is, of course, apodictic. The law dealing with release of slaves begins in
15:12. Its form is casuistic. Many commentators have noted

The question before us is whether there is any instance
of a prophetic accusation being grounded in casuistic law.
The problem is the probable allusion to the law of Deut.
15:12-18 in the PJS of Jer. 34:13-20. The issue is whether
the non-fulfillment of this Deuteronomic/casuistic law formed
the substance of Jeremiah's indictment. We think that it
did not.

A number of commentators have pointed to the difficulty
of reconciling what was apparently a general emancipation of
all slaves with the Deuteronomic requirement of a release of
a particular slave who had worked six years. The comment of
Rudolph is typical:

> . . . was damals geschah, war ein einmaliger Akt, der
> sich auf alle Schuldsklaven erstreckte, das Gesetz
> dagegen verlangte ihre Freilassung jeweils nach 6
> Dienstjahren, so dass solche Entlassungen je nach dem
> Dienstantritt fortwährend vorkamen. Und selbst wenn
> man annehmen wollte, das Gesetz sei lange nicht
> eingehalten worden (vgl. 14b), so dass jetzt auf einmal
> alle, die 6 und mehr Dienstjahre hatten, zur Entlassung
> kamen, so waren doch all die, die weniger als 6 Jahre
> in der Schuldsklaverei waren, dabei nicht in Frage
> gekommen.[1]

---

that the law of Ex. 21:2-6 does not apply to female slaves.

[1] Jeremia, p. 189. Cp. Bewer (The Prophets, p. 268) and
J. Philip Hyatt, "Jeremiah and Deuteronomy," JNES, I (April,
1942), p. 171. Blank (Jeremiah, p. 47), Bright (Jeremiah,
pp. 223-24), and H. H. Rowley in "The Prophet Jeremiah and
the Book of Deuteronomy," Studies in Old Testament Prophecy,
ed. by Rowley (Edinburgh: T. & T. Clark, 1950), p. 169,
account for the general manumission on the grounds of a ne-
glect of the law for many years. Bright alone of these
attempts to account for the release of those slaves who had
not yet completed six years service. Since he here follows

But, if one were to conclude from the difficulty in
reconciling the event reported in the Jeremiah passage with
the Deuteronomic law that the apparent reference to the law
is secondary, how is Zedekiah's proclamation to be explained?[1] Either or both of the following might have provided the motivation:

1. It was tactically expedient.

> Because of the siege the work of the slaves in the
> fields outside the city was impossible and they became
> an economic liability. In addition, as free men they
> could be asked to take an active share in the defence
> of the city.[2]

2. It might be religiously expedient; that is, a benevolent

act on the part of king and people might promote an equally

A. S. Peake in _Jeremiah and Lamentations, The New-Century
Bible_, II (New York: Henry Frowde, n.d.), p. 139, it is
Peake whom we will quote: "Now it is quite probable that the
law had for a considerable time been disregarded, and that
many had been in servitude for longer than six years. But it
is also probable that the term fixed by law had in many cases
not expired. It is therefore a plausible inference that the
reference to the law is due to an editor. It is possible,
however, that the emancipation was undertaken in obedience to
the neglected law; and that to make their action even more
effective, and perhaps atone for their earlier disregard,
they decided to emancipate all their slaves without waiting
till the legal term had expired." It is to be noted that
Peake straddles the fence between the possibility that the
people were following Deuteronomic law and the possibility
that the Deuteronomic reference is an insertion in the text
of Jeremiah.

[1]Among those who hold the Deuteronomic reference to be
a later insertion are Rudolph (_Jeremia_, p. 189) and Hyatt
("Jeremiah and Deuteronomy," p. 171).

[2]H. Cunliffe-Jones, _The Book of Jeremiah_ (London: SCM,
1960) p. 214. Cp. Blank, Jeremiah, p. 47.

benevolent response on the part of God:

> . . . by such a costly surrender (the freeing of the
> slaves) the masters hoped to win the help of Yahweh
> against Babylon.[1]

(In this context, it is interesting to note that an Old Babylonian document gives evidence that "the proclamation of a
release (of distrained persons) was regarded as pleasing the
gods"; which notion Jer. 34:15 also intimates:[2]

> But you have just turned around and done what pleased
> me by proclaiming liberty . . .

However,   ותעשו את־הישר בעיני   is typical Deuteronomic

---

[1]Peake, Jeremiah II, p. 139.

[2]The quoted words are from p. 28 of Julius Lewy's
"The Biblical Institution of Dᵉror in the Light of Akkadian Documents," Eretz-Israel, V (Jerusalem: The Israel Ex-
ploration Society and The Hebrew University, 1958), pp. 21-
31. The Akkadian documents show that the release of distrained persons was effected in either of two ways: by
". . . special action on the part of the administrative or
judicial authorities . . ." in accordance with a law which
limited servitude for debt to a period of three years; or by
a general release established by ". . . various Old Babylonian rulers of Amorite descent . . . by which the servitude
of many free-born persons came simultaneously to an end"
(p. 27). Of these two ways of effecting release, Lewy com-
pares the incident reported in Jeremiah with the former:
"Just as the Babylonian law-giver terminates the servitude of
the defaulting debtor and his family by the 'establishing of
their andurarum,' king Zedekiah and his subjects are said to
have agreed upon the 'proclamation of dᵉror for them' in
order to terminate the servitude of the 'Hebrew servants' who,
in violation of the law transmitted to us in Ex. 21:2 ff. and
Deut. 15:12 ff., had not been permitted 'to go out free'"
(fn. 53, pp. 26-27). Since, however, the originality of the
reference in Jeremiah 34:14 to the Deuteronomic law is in
doubt, and since Zedekiah's release seems to affect all
slaves, we would suggest that it is the second means of effecting release which illumines the incident related in
Jeremiah.

phraseology and may be editorial.[1])

But, if the Deuteronomic/casuistic law did not actually play a role in the incident we have been discussing, what was it that provoked Jeremiah's angry words of judgment?

We would reconstruct the situation as follows: With Jerusalem in a state of siege, Zedekiah issued an emancipation proclamation, which was ratified by a covenant ceremony. After the withdrawal of the Babylonian army (cp. Jer. 37:6-15), the slaves were brought back into subjection. This broke the covenant, whereupon Jeremiah intervened with a PJS, the gist of which may be inferred from 34:17-20 (the words are ours, not his): "Because you pledged liberty, but did not uphold that pledge--liberty shall be yours . . . ; because the covenant was not fulfilled, the curse of the covenant will be effected upon those who were party to it."[2] That is, it was breach of covenant, and it alone, that evoked Jeremiah's indictment. Why does he mention the disregarded

---

[1]S. R. Driver, An Introduction to the Literature of the Old Testament (New York: Meridian Books, 1956), p. 101, lists the phrase as typical of Deuteronomic style. However, this does not preclude Jeremiah's having said it. Such Deuteronomic language may be accounted for either on the ground that Jeremiah knew Deuteronomy, or on the ground of a common terminology of the time. Cp. Rowley ("Jeremiah and Deuteronomy," p. 170) and Hyatt ("Jeremiah and Deuteronomy," pp. 164-65).

[2]For the point that each of the human participants in the covenant ceremony took upon himself a "conditional curse"; see Blank, Jeremiah, p. 48.

proclamation? Since the covenant had both a _form_ (the passing between the parts of the calf by those who were party to the covenant) and a _content_ (the proclamation of liberty), Jeremiah's AD (34:17-20) makes reference to both.[1]

That the breaking of a covenant is, in itself, quite enough to draw prophetic accusation and divine punishment is seen in a passage from Jeremiah's contemporary, Ezekiel (17:1-21).[2] Zedekiah (here unnamed), who seems to have had a penchant for covenant-breaking, is again the principal. Having renounced his allegiance to Nebuchadrezzar, and with Jerusalem under siege by the Babylonians as a result, Zedekiah has appealed to Egypt for aid.[3] Ezekiel responds with

---

[1]Volz misinterprets the references in Jeremiah's AD to the disregarded proclamation _and_ the broken covenant as signifying a double transgression: "Die Strafe wird zum Vergehen in Beziehung gesetzt, und weil das Vergehen ein doppeltes ist (gegen die Nebenmenschen und gegen die Religion), wird auch die Strafe doppelt ausgedrückt: 1. weil sie den Nebenmenschen die Freilassung nicht hielten, sollen sie freigelassen werden: für den Tod; 2. weil sie den zwischen den Stücken des Kalbs geschworenen Eid nicht hielten, sollen ihre Leichen von Tieren verzehrt werden" (_Jeremia_, p. 322).

[2]Other examples of the breach of a covenant as forming the basis for prophetic accusation and divine punishment are to be found in Amos 1. See Michael Fishbane, "The Treaty Background of Amos 1:11 and Related Matters," _JBL_, LXXXIX (September, 1970), pp. 313-18.

[3]For the historical background, see Martin Noth, _The History of Israel_, trans. by Stanley Godman (New York: Harper & Brothers, 1958), pp. 283-85. Cp., also, Blank, _Jeremiah_, pp. 37-39.

an allegory and its interpretation, the following portions of
the interpretation being sufficient for our purpose:[1]

> The king of Babylon came to Jerusalem, and took her king
> (Jehoiachin) and her princes and deported them to Baby-
> lon. Then he took one of the royal progeny (Zedekiah)
> and made a covenant with him, bringing him under oath
> . . . But he rebelled against him by sending ambas-
> sadors to Egypt (with the hope of) procuring horses and
> a large army. Will he be successful? Can one who does
> such things escape? Can he break a covenant and go
> free? . . . Therefore thus says the Lord God: So help
> me, (for) my oath which he despised and my covenant
> which he broke, I'll requite him.
> (17:12-13, 15, 19)

As in Jeremiah 34, so here, the breaking of a covenant is a
sole and sufficient ground for prophetic accusation.[2]

Finally, it is to be noted that our view that breach of
covenant forms the basis of Jeremiah's accusation is consonant with the prophet's thought as a whole; for its obverse
is the Jeremianic emphasis upon faithfulness as a virtue in

---

[1]Many commentators consider vss. 16-18 to be secondary.
E.g., Walther Eichrodt, Ezekiel, trans. by Cosslett Quin
(London: SCM, 1970), p. 226; John W. Wevers, Ezekiel, The
Century Bible, New Series (Aylesbury: Nelson, 1969), p. 136.
Eichrodt (p. 226) argues that the interpretation, as well as
the allegory, is to be attributed to Ezekiel. It is interesting that Ezekiel sees Zedekiah's refusal to remain sub-
missive to the Babylonians as a covenant matter; while Jeremiah emphasizes that Babylonian domination and Judah's sub-
servience are matters of God's will (Jer. 27:1-8; 28:14).
Eichrodt (Ezekiel, pp. 226-27) seems to worry about this and
struggles to "reconcile" the two views.

[2]N.B. As was Jeremiah's AD (see p. 72, above), so
Ezekiel's accusation is couched in terms of content ("my
oath which he despised") and form ("my covenant which he
broke").

and of itself.[1]

Prime evidence of this theme is Jeremiah's commend-
ation of the Rechabites:

> . . . because you kept the charge of Jonadab your fa-
> ther, and obeyed all his commandments, doing every-
> thing he has commanded you, therefore thus says the
> Lord of hosts, the God of Israel: Jonadab ben Rechab
> shall never lack a man to stand in my service.
> (35:18-19)

That is, just as he here commends the Rechabites for their
faithfulness and announces their reward; so, in 34:17-20,
does Jeremiah condemn the people for their unfaithfulness
and announce their punishment.

We have wondered whether a passage could be found in
which a prophet's accusation was grounded in casuistic law.
We have now examined the one passage where such might have
been the case, but have seen that breach of covenant was the
real basis of the prophet's charge. Therefore, we may go on
to say: where law is the basis of a prophetic accusation,
such accusation is grounded solely in apodictic law.

Might one infer from this, and as the reason for it,
that the prophets did not know casuistic law? This is
hardly the case! Jeremiah, himself, is a prime witness:

If a man divorces his wife and she leaves him and

---

[1]Cp. Blank, Jeremiah, p. 175; Hammershaimb, "Ethics,"
p. 97.

76

marries another, can she return to him[1] again? Wouldn't
that land be greatly polluted? But, as for you, you
have whored around with many lovers; can you return to
me? . . . (3:1)[2]

Look, now, at Deut. 24:1-4:

Suppose that (כי) a man takes a woman and marries her,
and it happens that (אם) she displeases him because he
has found in her some impropriety, whereupon he writes
her a bill of divorce and, placing it in her hand, sends
her from his house. Leaving his house, she goes and
becomes the wife of another and, because the latter
comes to dislike her, he writes her a bill of divorce
and, placing it in her hand, sends her from his house;
or else, the latter fellow who took her as his wife
dies. (In such a case) her former husband who dismissed her cannot, again, take her to be his wife after
she has become defiled; for that is an abhorrence to the
Lord--you must not let the land incur guilt . . .

Jeremiah, then, does know casuistic law. However, casuistic

law is here used not as the ground for an accusation (the

accusation is apostasy, characterized as adultery); but, it

is used metaphorically, to query whether reconciliation is

possible.[3]

Jeremiah 2:34 also contains a reference to casuistic

law:

---

[1]Cp. Rudolph, _Jeremia_, p. 20: (read) ". . . wegen lb*β*
mit LXX השוב אליו ."

[2]On the genuineness of this verse, see Hyatt, "Jeremiah and Deuteronomy," p. 164. One should not, a priori,
pronounce every Deuteronomic reference secondary in Jeremiah; one must first establish the secondary nature of such
a passage on other grounds. (cp. fn. 1, p. 71)

[3]For the content of the accusation, see Bright (_Jer-
emiah_, p. 25) and Rudolph (_Jeremia_, p. 21); for Jeremiah's
metaphor and query, see Blank (_Jeremiah_, p. 182).

. . . on your skirts is found the blood of innocent
souls;[1] you did not find them breaking in . . .

That to which Jeremiah alludes is found in Ex. 22:1:

If a thief is caught breaking in, and is struck so that
he dies, there shall be no bloodguilt for him.

While the Hebrew text of Jer. 2:34 is difficult, and it is
not clear who the "innocent souls" are (perhaps אביונים was
an insertion whose purpose was to clear up this difficulty),
the point of the reference to casuistic law is not to ground
the accusation, but to establish culpability.[2]

A final example, showing that prophets (and not Jeremiah alone) were not unaware of casuistic law, is Isaiah
4:1:

And seven women will take hold of one man on that day,
saying, "Our own food we'll eat and our own clothes
we'll wear, if you'll only let us be called by your
name; take away our reproach."

The import of Isaiah's message is clarified by Ex. 21:10
(In context, the verse refers to a concubine and her rights
upon her master's taking "another" concubine/wife.[3] However, if a master must provide these things for a slave
girl--קל וחמר--how much more, a husband for his wife.):

---

[1]Omitting אביונים with LXX.

[2]Rudolph (Jeremia, p. 18) thinks that the "innocent
souls" are the "prophets" of vs. 30b. The concern of the law
in Ex. 22:1-2a is to determine liability; Jeremiah is saying,
"You are liable."

[3]The Hebrew of 21:10a is אם־אחרת יקח־לו. Has he taken
another concubine, or has he married?

78

> If he marries another, he shall not withhold her (his
> concubine's) food, her clothing, or her oil.[1]

Isaiah is saying, then, that Jerusalem's formerly proud

women will be so desperate that they'll forego that to which

any wife (or even a concubine) is entitled, just to get a

husband. Once again, an accusation is not involved in an

apparent allusion to casuistic law.

We have now examined instances where casuistic law:

1) forms the basis of a prophetic metaphor (Jer. 3:1); 2) is

used to obviate a plea of extenuating circumstances (Jer. 2:

34); 3) stands behind a prophet's imagery (Is. 4:1). Yet,

it is not used to ground prophetic accusation. So far as we

are able to ascertain, it is apodictic laws alone to which

prophetic accusation attributes binding force. But, if "The

Law in the Prophets" is apodictic law, on what grounds do the

prophets understand these laws to be binding?

---

[1]Shalom M. Paul, "Exod. 21:10 a Threefold Maintenance
Clause," _JNES_, 28 (January, 1969), pp. 48-53, has shown from
extra-biblical evidence that, whatever the "ultimate etymo-
logical derivation" of עֹנָה, it "appears to be an otherwise unknown equivalent for 'oil, ointments'" (p. 52).

II: THE AUTHORITY OF THE LAW IN THE PROPHETS

If one were to think of men like Nathan, Elijah, and
their successors among the writing prophets as hunting-dogs
on the trail of quarry (those who have transgressed apodictic
law), while the image would not be exhaustive of the prophetic function, it would certainly be apropos of one aspect
of it. Like a hunter, they are sent; and, upon finding their
quarry, they point: "Thou art the man." For the object of
the prophetic pursuit to be fair game, however, the law(s)
which has (have) been transgressed must be valid. Our
present task is to inquire into the grounds on which the
prophets understood such law to be binding--to seek the
authority of the law in the prophets.

For a law to be binding, two conditions are necessary:
1) it has to have been enacted; and 2) it has to be enforced.[1]
That is, there is both a legislative and an executive aspect
to a law's authority. The banks in our country are protected by law from robbery. Since this law was enacted by

---

[1]Cp. *Webster's New World Dictionary of the American
Language: College Edition* (Cleveland and New York: The
World Publishing Company, 1958), p. 828: ". . . law, in
its specific application, implies prescription and enforcement by a ruling authority . . ."

80

Congress, we designate it, from a legislative standpoint, a Congressional law. On the other hand, since the process leading to the apprehension and punishment of those who break this law is undertaken by agents of the Federal Government, this law is, from an executive standpoint, a Federal law. It is one law, but each designation emphasizes a different aspect of the law's authority.

This dual aspect of authority is to be found in the prophetic understanding of the law: for them, the law is binding because it has a legislative framework; and, it is binding because those who break it will be punished.[1] Since it will yield more easily to our investigation, we will begin by looking at the question of the law's enforcement.

The Authority of the Law: The Executive Aspect

We start with a question: "Who, according to the prophets, takes responsibility for punishing those who transgress the law?" It is clear that the prophets see the enforcement of the law as the work of God. Our first witness is the PJS. I Kings 21:18-19 is a typical example:[2]

---

[1]We make no claim that terminology such as "executive aspect" or "legislative framework," which we are using with reference to the law, would have made sense to the prophets; but, it helps us understand in what sense the law was authoritative for them.

[2]The PJS has been considered in detail in our discussion of Westermann's Grundformen on pp. 7-26, above. For the abbreviations used throughout this paper to designate the

Commissioning of the Messenger:	Get along down to meet Ahab . . . and say to him
Accusation:	"Have you committed murder, and also taken possession?"
Messenger Formula:	"Thus says the Lord:
Announcement of Disaster:	In the place where the dogs lapped Naboth's blood will dogs lap your blood--yes, yours."

Let us note the following:

1. The crimes which Ahab is accused of committing are in violation of the apodictic laws prohibiting murder and coveting.[1]

2. Since it is God who commissions the messenger, it is he who initiates the process, the result of which is the punishment of the transgressor. Just as the Federal Government sends out the F.B.I. when a Federal crime has been committed; so God sends forth his agents, the prophets, when apodictic law has been transgressed.

It is necessary to observe, however, that especially in the Judgment-Speeches of the literary prophets, the CM is more conspicuous by its absence than its presence. This is to be explained by the fact that it is not, in reality, a part of the PJS itself; but only an indication of what

---

Prophetic Judgment-Speech and its parts, see p. vii.

[1]We have discussed at length this accusation and its basis in apodictic law in fn. 3 on pp. 63-64, above.

motivates that speech.[1] As such, the CM only appears when
the speech is transmitted in a narrative context (e.g., Jer.
7:2; 27:13; Is. 22:15). On the other hand, all Prophetic
Judgment-Speeches may be understood as initiated by God in
the sense that the prophetic call stands behind all the words
of a prophet (e.g., Amos 7:15; Is. 6:8-9; Jer. 1:7; cp.,
also, Mic. 3:8 which grounds the prophet's accusations in
"the spirit of the Lord"). Thus, whether by immediate commission or by the prophet's call, God sets in motion the
process which leads to the punishment of those who transgress
the law.

3. The effective power of the word is a well-known aspect
of the biblical "Weltanschauung."[2] Since the word is

---

[1]The formal "home" of the CM is what Westermann
(Grundformen, pp. 71-72) calls "Die Botensendung." While the
CM is formally independent of the PJS, Westermann rightly
includes it, for the fact that it introduces that speech when
it is transmitted in a narrative context shows its intimate
connection with it. Klaus Koch (Biblical Tradition, p. 191)
prefers the term "private oracle" to CM, because "exactly the
same formula, with the two imperatives, crops up in situations which do not call for a message but merely another
duty" (e.g. II Kings 1:15). Koch's term is helpful, because
it explains why the CM is absent when the PJS appears without a narrative context--the "commissioning" is a private
matter between the prophet and God. However, Koch keeps his
formal integrity only by foregoing the crucial point: "Get
along down to meet Ahab . . . and say to him . . ." indicates
that the PJS originates in the command of God.

[2]Cp. J. N. Sanders, "Word, the," IDB, IV, p. 869:
"That power should be attributed to God's word is not surprising, but it is also attributed to the words of men . . .
A word once uttered takes on a life of its own beyond the
control of the speaker and achieves its effect by a kind of

83

effective, and since, in the PJS, the MF stipulates that the
AD (the punishment prescribed for the transgression) is God's
word, therefore, God is the author of the punishment. Further, in a number of instances where an AD is joined to an
Ac. whose content is the transgression of apodictic law, God
declares (through the mouth of the prophet) that he, himself,
will be agent as well as author of the punitive action.
Micah 2:1-4 is a typical example:[1]

> Woe to the plotters of iniquity,
> Those who lie abed scheming evil!
> At daylight they effect it,
> For the power is theirs.
> When they covet fields, they seize them;
> If houses, they take them.
> They oppress a man and his house,
> A man and his inheritance.
> Therefore thus says the Lord:
> Be sure that I'm going to plot evil against
>   this family,
> From which you'll not remove your necks
> . . .

That the behavior of the accused was contrary to several

apodictic laws (Ex. 20:17; Lev. 19:13; Deut. 27:17) has been

---

innate power."

[1]Other passages according to which God directly involves himself in punishing those who transgress apodictic
law include: Amos 2:6-8, 13-16; 5:11-13, 16-17; Is. 31:1-3;
Jer. 7:8-10, 14; 13:25-27 (26). The underlined verse(s) in
each example indicates the divine agency. For apodictic law
as the basis of Amos' accusations in these passages, see
Bach, "Gottesrecht," pp. 26-33. For Jer. 7:9, see pp. 60-62,
above. The behavior condemned in Is. 31:1 and Jer. 13:25
contravenes Ex. 20:3, while that of Jer. 13:27 is prohibited
by Ex. 20:4-5a and 22:19.

pointed out by Beyerlin.[1] What we note is that God will,
himself, effect punishment ("I'm going to plot evil . . ."),
tit for tat, against those who have transgressed the law.

To summarize: the PJS shows that, 1) where an accusation entails the breaking of apodictic law, 2) God initiates the punitive action by sending an agent to assert that
transgression has occurred and to announce the consequent
disaster and, 3) that word which effects punishment (the AD),
being designated by the MF as God's word, points to God as
the author of the punishment. Moreover, the AD often indicates God as the punitive agent. Thus the PJS stands as a
witness that the prophets understand that God takes the
responsibility for punishing those who transgress the law.

A further witness to the prophetic understanding that
it is God who acts to enforce the law is the so-called "lawsuit of God."[2] In the usual form of the "lawsuit," God acts

---

[1]Kulttraditionen, p. 57.

[2]The "lawsuit" literature includes: Berend Gemser,
"The Rîb--or Controversy--Pattern in Hebrew Mentality,"
Adhuc Loquitur, ed. by A. van Selms and A. S. van der Woude
(Leiden: E. J. Brill, 1968), pp. 116-37; Julien Harvey, Le
Plaidoyer prophétique contre Israël après la rupture de
l'alliance (Bruges: Desclée de Brouwer and Montréal: Les
Éditions Bellarmin, 1967); Delbert R. Hillers, Covenant: The
History of a Biblical Idea (Baltimore: The Johns Hopkins
Press, 1969), pp. 124-31; Herbert B. Huffmon, "The Covenant
Lawsuit in the Prophets," JBL, LXXVIII (December, 1959), pp.
285-95; James Limburg, "The Root ריב and the Prophetic Lawsuit
Speeches," JBL, LXXXVIII (September, 1969), pp. 291-304; G.
Ernest Wright, "The Lawsuit of God: A Form-Critical Study of
Deuteronomy 32," Israel's Prophetic Heritage, pp. 26-67;

as plaintiff and accuses the defendant, Israel.[1] While the accusation contained in Jer. 2:4-13 involves more than just the breaking of a law, it is equally clear that Israel's behavior is contrary to what the law enjoins. In the relevant portion of the accusation, God says:

> What disability did your fathers find in me
> That they abandoned me
> To follow Nothingness, thereby gaining nothing?[2]
> . . .
> Therefore I will still make a complaint against you--
>   it is the Lord speaking--
> And against your children's children will I make a
>   complaint.[3]
> Journey to the Cypriot coasts and see
> Send to Kedar and consider carefully . . .
> Whether a nation has changed gods,
> Though gods they aren't--
> Yet my people has changed its glory
> For that which avails nought.
> . . . Two evils my people have perpetrated:
> They have abandoned me,
> A fountain of living waters,
> To hew out cisterns for themselves,
> Broken cisterns,

Ernst Würthwein, "Der Ursprung der prophetischen Gerichts-rede," ZThK, 49 (1952), pp. 1-16.

[1]Cp. Huffmon, "Covenant Lawsuit," pp. 285-86.

[2]The translation is difficult, because three things must be held in balance: 1) the pun (ההבל ויהבלו); 2) the people think they are following real gods; 3) the prophet declares them to be ineffective. We try to reproduce the pun by "Nothingness . . . nothing"; and to capture the presumed divinity of these "gods" (and Jeremiah's irony) by the capital N; and the prophet's assertion of their ineffectiveness by the word "nothingness."

[3]For "make a complaint against" as the proper translation of ריב את in 2:9, see Limburg, "ריב," p. 301.

Which cannot hold[1] water (2:5, 9-13).

Though apostasy is forbidden by apodictic law (Ex. 20:3;
22:19; 34:13a), Israel has become apostate. Just as the
government prosecutes those who break Federal law, so here,
God goes to court--clearly expressing the divine determination to enforce the law.

The "lawsuit" affords a further example of such divine
determination. In this instance, however, as James Limburg
has shown, ". . . Yahweh is not accuser of his people, but
rather advocate for them."[2]

> The Lord is taking his place to make accusation,
> He is standing to judge nations.[3]
> The Lord enters into judgment
> With the elders and princes of his people.
> "You there! You have depastured[4] the vineyard,

---

[1]Following the suggestion of Rudolph (Jeremia, p. 12)
and reading יִכְלָא (from כלא) for יְכַלְכְּלוּ.

[2]"ריב," p. 303.

[3]Retaining the MT עַמִּים, with Limburg (" ריב," p. 303).
In Prophecy in Ancient Israel (Oxford: Basil Blackwell,
1962), Johannes Lindblom explains the passage thus: "In iii.
13 it is said that Yahweh is about to judge the peoples. In
the light of ii. 10 ff. the peoples . . . must be mankind,
not the tribes of Israel. The punishment of the elders and
princes of Judah is here regarded as an individual feature in
a general world judgment" (p. 366).

[4]"Depastured" is the translation of George Buchanan
Gray, A Critical and Exegetical Commentary on the Book of
Isaiah (Edinburgh: T & T Clark, 1912), p. 69. Gray has
caught the possible allusion to the casuistically formulated
law of Ex. 22:4. However, one should not confuse the imagery
in which an accusation is clothed with the content of the
accusation. As the second colon makes clear, the elders and
princes are accused of robbery.

What was robbed from the poor is in your houses.
What's with you that you crush my people,
That you grind the face of the poor? . . ."
(Is. 3:13-15)

God again goes to court; here, to defend his poor against
those who oppress them. The behavior here condemned is
similar to that indicted by Amos (3:10; 5:11; 8:4) and Micah
(3:2-3), and is prohibited, according to Lev. 19:13a: "You
must not oppress or rob your neighbor."

Thus do two prophets, by placing an accusation of
behavior contrary to apodictic law in the framework of a
"lawsuit of God," intimate the willingness of God to enforce
the law against those who transgress it.

We are trying to ascertain the prophetic understanding
of the authority of the law. To be sure, our question ("On
what grounds do you understand the law to be authoritative?")
is their assumption ("It is authoritative"). However, if one
side of the authority of law is enforcement, the PJS and the
"lawsuit of God" imply that, for the prophets, God is the
"enforcer": ferreting out offenders through his agents, the
prophets, entering into legal proceedings, and, himself, punishing the guilty.

Yet--lest we misunderstand--by cloaking a PJS in the
form of a lament, Isaiah helps us see that, lamentable as
is the transgression which prompts it, the punitive action

which it prompts is quite as painful to God:[1]

> Too bad that she has become a whore;
> A once faithful city
> Full of justice,
> In whom righteousness used to lodge--
> But now murderers.
> Your silver has become dross,
> Your spirits adulterated[2] with water.
> Your rulers are recalcitrant,
> Compatriots of thieves.
> Everyone loves a bribe,
> Pursues rewards.
> They don't do right by the orphan,
> Of the complaint of the widow they take
>   no account.
> Therefore--it is the Lord,
> The Lord of hosts,
> The Mighty One of Israel speaking--
> I am compelled to vent my wrath[3] on
>   my adversaries,
> Avenge myself on my enemies (1:21-24).

Punish God must, and punish he will, when the law is broken.

The law has teeth say the prophets; for God guarantees its

---

[1]For Is. 1:21-23 as an accusation composed as a lament, see Westermann, *Grundformen*, p. 144. Note the correspondence of the accusations to the injunctions of apodictic law: they are murderers (cp. Ex. 20:13); thieves (Ex. 20:15); they accept bribes (Deut. 16:19) and deny justice to the orphan and widow (Deut. 27:19).

[2]For the rendition "adulterated," see the philological note of Gray (*Isaiah*, pp. 35-36).

[3]One would wish, in translation, to render the pain and dissatisfaction expressed by חרה (cp. *BDB*, p. 222), as well as the compulsion of the אנחם. We have chosen to give emphasis to the latter, at the expense of the former. Sheldon Blank beautifully expressed the same divine pain/compulsion in a classroom exegesis of Jer. 45:4-5. My class notes read: "God's response to Baruch is, 'Don't think that I, God, am without distress.' Human grief is held up against divine grief. God, too, is capable of self-pity. The participle in 45:4 should be understood in a modal sense--'I must destroy'; i.e., God is subject to his own laws. God _can_ suffer. experience grief."

enforcement.

The Legislative Framework of the Law

    During the years of my pastoral ministry, I was accustomed to engage in pre-marital counselling with those at whose weddings I was to officiate. At some point during the first session the following conversation would occur:

Pastor: Why do you want to marry?

Couple: We're in love.

Pastor: How do you know?

Couple: It's this feeling . . .

After "this feeling" had been described to a greater or lesser degree, I would ask why "this feeling" was necessarily indicative of love rather than something else. At this point I would recall a series of lectures I had once heard which had attempted to distinguish love from infatuation. Going to a blackboard, I would place on one side the word "love," and on the other the word "infatuation"; and, under each, the words "this feeling." Then, in each column, I would begin to place certain features which--I had learned from the lectures--were characteristic of the one or the other. When the columns were completed, the lesson could be drawn: there is what might be called a "love" framework and an "infatuation" framework, and "this feeling" might be part of either; it is only by other features in conjunction with which our "this feeling" is found that we may know of which framework our "this feeling" is a part.

Our problem is similar to that which I posed for my
counsellees: we want to demonstrate the probability that,
for the prophets, the law (the item under consideration; cp.
"this feeling") was part of the covenant between Yahweh and
Israel whose form was that of a treaty (a particular system/
framework; cp. "love"). As I made available to my couples the
elements of the two systems so that they might compare with
them the data of their own experience, so we have materials
from which to elucidate covenants and their forms--non-
prophetic biblical material, Ancient Near Eastern treaty
texts, and significant secondary literature--with which we
may compare the data from our prophetic texts.[1]

It was George Mendenhall in his seminal study, Law and
Covenant in Israel and the Ancient Near East, who showed how
various elements characteristic of the Hittite treaty texts
find parallels in the biblical materials, indicating that the

---

[1]For the treaty texts themselves, see the bibliography
of Dennis McCarthy, Treaty and Covenant, pp. xiii-xiv. Basic
secondary literature includes, in addition to McCarthy:
Klaus Baltzer, Das Bundesformular (Neukirchen: Neukirchener
Verlag, 1960); Delbert R. Hillers, Covenant, op. cit., and
Treaty-Curses and the Old Testament Prophets (Rome: Pontif-
ical Biblical Institute, 1964); George E. Mendenhall,
"Covenant," IDB, I, pp. 714-23, and Law and Covenant, op. cit.
James Muilenburg, "The Form and Structure of the Covenantal
Formulations," VT, IX (October, 1959), pp. 347-65. For an
opposing view, see Erhard Gerstenberger, "Covenant and
Commandment," JBL, LXXXIV (March, 1965), pp. 38-51.

biblical traditions were not unaware of the treaty form of covenant.[1] Of special interest is Mendenhall's view that the Decalogue represents the "stipulations" imposed by Yahweh on the new covenant community at Sinai; that is, in the Sinai pericope, the law is the text of the covenant.[2] While this has been disputed by Dennis McCarthy, the latter's examination of the "central discourse" in Deuteronomy (4:44-28:68) sees it as clearly exemplifying the treaty form; the legal material of 12-26:15 representing the treaty stipulations, being "in its proper place in the sequence of the treaty structure, between the introduction (4:44-11:32) and the blessings and curses (26:16-28:68)."[3] These studies having demonstrated the presence of an awareness of the treaty form in the biblical material and that, possibly in the Sinai material and certainly in Deuteronomy, the law is to be

---

[1]Op. cit., pp. 24-50, passim. We have summarized this part of Mendenhall's study on pp. 35-36, above.

[2]Law and Covenant, p. 37. Mendenhall makes the same point in "Covenant," p. 719: ". . . it is possible to identify the Decalogue as the original text of the covenant between Yahweh and Israel, though in its present form it has undergone some expansion and interpretation."

[3]For McCarthy's argument that the "central discourse" in Deuteronomy exemplifies the treaty form, see ch. 9 of Treaty and Covenant. The quotation is from p. 120. We have set out McCarthy's criticism of Mendenhall on pp. 37-40, above. Our problem, of course, is not whether any particular group of laws was, in its origin, covenant stipulations; but whether the prophets understood the laws which underlie prophetic accusation to be covenant stipulations.

understood within this covenant context--_it becomes at least possible that the prophets, too, viewed the law as a component of such a covenant framework_.

How shall we proceed? Just as from the presence of a number of features characteristic of the "love" framework a couple might infer that "this feeling" which they shared was indicative of love, so, from the presence of a number of elements characteristic of Ancient Near Eastern treaties and/ or biblical covenant documents which, in the prophetic material, are joined to allusions to the law (e.g., to a prophetic accusation whose content is behavior contrary to apodictic law), we may infer that, for the prophets, the law was part of a covenant whose form was that of a treaty. Thus our procedure will be to examine the prophetic material for such "covenant elements" in conjunction with legal allusions.

We must interject a note of caution: those who are interested in demonstrating an hypothesis are always in danger of falling prey to a propensity for eisegesis. Having been apprised of the elements of the "love" framework, a couple will begin an avid search of their experience for the presence of these elements and will not be above distorting events to "find" them therein. We have tried to minimize the possibility of our being similarly susceptible. For the "covenant elements" in the prophetic material we have relied on the generally accepted work of our predecessors, while for demonstrating the relationship of legal allusions to these elements we have depended on accepted canons of form-critical exegesis.[1]

Let us be aware, also, that we are dealing with probabilities, not proof. Our situation is analogous to that of a physician. From the presence of certain symptoms he must attempt a diagnosis. Individual symptoms, or even two or three together, may point in more than one direction. Nevertheless, as the symptoms are accumulated, one answer begins to emerge as the more probable. So with us. It is the accumulation of covenant elements to which legal allusions are joined that confirms for us the probability of a treaty context.

One may, of course, ask: "Why must the elements be part of a framework? Surely a word such as '. . . the corpses of this people will become food for the carrion birds and wild beasts, with no one to frighten them away' (Jer. 7: 33), is about as meaningful as any word could be." Our answer would be that the individual features of the prophetic message gain <u>their</u> <u>full</u> <u>meaning</u> only when they are seen as part of a larger context. For example, the formal connection between a prophet's Ac. and the AD becomes sensible only when we understand that the announced disaster is punishment for

---

[1]This will be substantiated in the text and footnotes as our argument proceeds.

the behavior of the accused, that behind the formal connection stands a logical connection. And, it is precisely
the framework which provides the logical connection.

Let us, then, proceed with our hypothesis that, for
the prophets, the law was part of the covenant and examine
material from those prophets who are our special concern
(Amos, Micah, Isaiah, and Jeremiah) to see if we can find
any "covenant elements" in conjunction with legal allusions.

Announcements of Disaster whose contents parallel treaty-
curses and/or curses in biblical curse lists are connected
in the prophetic material with accusations of behavior which
is contrary to apodictic law

In the fourth chapter of his monograph, Treaty-Curses
and the Old Testament Prophets, Delbert R. Hillers collects
a number of "parallels in specific details" between treaty-
curses and "the prophetic oracles of doom."[1] What is of interest to us is that, several times, these curse-parallels
form part of an AD which is related to an accusation of
behavior contrary to apodictic law. Of the prophets within
our purview, Jeremiah affords a clear majority of such
instances.[2]

---

[1]Op. cit., pp. 43-79. Cp., also, Hillers' Covenant,
pp. 131-40. What Hillers calls "oracles of doom," we have
called Announcements of Disaster.

[2]Of the places where a treaty-curse parallel is joined
to an accusation of behavior contrary to apodictic law, we
list below only those passages where the connection seems
clear. In each case we list, in order, the page(s) (from

Jeremiah 7:30-34 is one example. (This passage is similar in content to 19:2b-9, 11b-13. Volz considers 7:30-34 a collection of verses from several chapters. Bright, Peake, and Rudolph judge 7:30-34 to be original, while they call the passage in chapter 19 an expansion. Hyatt considers both passages to be the work of Deuteronomic editors.[1] For our part, while neither may be "original,"--i.e., contain the ipsissima verba of the prophet--both are "genuine," in that

---

Treaty-Curses) where Hillers discusses the particular curse, his designation for the curse, and the prophetic reference(s). Only the verses which contain the treaty-curse parallel are listed. The Ac. which gives rise to the AD/treaty-curse parallel usually precedes it in the text.

p. 29	"'Futility' Curses"	Amos 5:11 (cp. Deut. 28:30)
		Mic. 3:4; 6:14-15
pp. 54-56	"Devouring animals"	Jer. 5:6
pp. 57-58	"Removal of joyful sounds"	Jer. 7:34; 25:10
pp. 58-60	"To be stripped like a prostitute"	Jer. 13:26
pp. 62-63	"To eat the flesh of sons and daughters"	Jer. 19:9 (cp. Deut. 28:53-57)
pp. 63-64	"Contaminated water"	Jer. 23:15
pp. 68-69	"No burial"	Is. 5:25
		Jer. 7:33; 8:1-2; 19:7; 22:19 (cp. Deut. 28:26)
pp. 70-71	"Flood"	Is. 8:7
pp. 76-77	"Passers-by will shudder"	Mic. 6:16
		Jer. 18:16; 19:8; 25:9

[1]For the views here referred to, see: Bright, Jeremiah, pp. 131, 133; Hyatt, "Jeremiah and Deuteronomy," p. 167; Peake, Jeremiah, I, p. 236; Rudolph, Jeremia, pp. 50-51, 109; Volz, Jeremia, pp. 105, 201-4.

they recall the gist of a PJS containing a specific accusation together with an AD, the contents of which are paralleled in treaty-curses. What was "original" to Jeremiah
was an Ac. whose content was similar to that of 7:30-31 and
19:4-5 followed by an AD whose content was similar to treaty-
curses; and this, the tradition has rightly "remembered."[1]
First, the accusation:

> The inhabitants of Judah have done me wrong--it is the
> Lord speaking--they have set up their detestable things
> in the house which is called by my name, profaning it
> thereby. And they have built the high places of
> Topheth, which is in the valley of Ben-hinnom, to burn
> their sons and daughters in the fire; which I did not
> command--indeed, it never occurred to me (7:30-31).

The people are accused of idolatry and child sacrifice (cp.
19:4-5). Each is prohibited by apodictic law; the former by
Ex. 20:4-5a (cp. Deut. 5:8-9a), the latter by Lev. 18:21
(cp. Deut. 18:10a). Because of this behavior, disaster is

---

[1]We agree with Bright (_Jeremiah_, pp. 58-59) in the
comment which he appends to his discussion of 7:1-8:3: "The
prose discourses of Jeremiah, as their stereotyped style
indicates, do not provide us--at least, not consistently--
with the prophet's _ipsissima verba_, but rather preserve the
gist of what he said as that was remembered and repeated by
his followers. We have, therefore, in evaluating them to
reckon with verbal expansion, and even with the possibility
of some adaptation, of the prophet's thought. But there is
no reason to question the essential authenticity of this
material, which is, for the most part, fully in his spirit."
Cp., also, Bright, "The Date of the Prose Sermons of Jeremiah," _JBL_, LXX (1951), p. 27. Thus, with regard to 7:30-34
and 19:2b-9, while either or (to a greater or lesser extent)
both may exhibit editorial creativity; we are dealing with
"creatio ex Jeremia," rather than, as Hyatt would have it
("Jeremiah and Deuteronomy," p. 167), "creatio ex Deuter-
onomium."

97

certain:

> Therefore you can be sure that days are coming--it is
> the Lord speaking--when this place will no longer be
> spoken of as Topheth, or the valley of Ben-hinnom,
> but as the valley of Slaughter . . . And the corpses
> of this people will become food for the carrion birds
> and wild beasts, with no one to frighten them away. And
> I will extinguish from the cities of Judah and the
> streets of Jerusalem the sound of joy and the sound of
> gladness, the voice of the bridegroom and the voice of
> the bride; for the land will become a ruin (7:32-34).

The content of the disaster which Jeremiah here announces is
similar to that of the treaty-curses which Hillers has
called, "no burial" and "removal of joyful sounds."[1] A curse
from the Esarhaddon treaty, 426-27, is an example of the
former: "May he give your flesh to the vulture (and) jackal
to devour."[2] A curse invoking "the removal of joyful sounds'
occurs in the Sefire treaty, I A 29: "Nor may the sound of
the lyre be heard in Arpad and among its people."[3]

In addition to 7:30-34, the conjunction, in Jeremiah,
of an Ac. of some form of apostasy with an AD whose content
parallels treaty-curses is frequent, and should be understood

---

[1]_Treaty-Curses_, pp. 68-69 and 57-58, respectively. For
the treaty-curse parallels to Jer. 19:7-9, see fn. 2, pp. 93-
94, above.

[2]_Ibid._, p. 68. Other examples of "no burial" curses
along with biblical parallels, will be found on pp. 68-69.
It should be noted that the content of 7:33 appears in the
curse-list of Deut. 28 (vs. 26) and in Jer. 34:20. Hillers
sees it as "one of the most common of traditional curses,
certainly not the invention of Jeremiah or the author of
Deut. 28" (p. 33).

[3]_Ibid._, p. 57. Other examples and biblical parallels

as characteristic of the prophet (cp. 8:1-2; 13:26-27; 18:13-17; 23:13-15; 25:6, 9-10).[1]

However, it is not only apostasy which draws Announcements of Disaster whose contents parallel treaty-curses. Such announcements also follow accusations of other transgressions of apodictic law. A passage from Jeremiah affords a clear example; Jehoiakim here being the object of the prophet's Judgment-Speech:

> Woe to the one who builds his house by unrighteousness
> And his upper chambers by injustice;
> Who makes his neighbor work for him for nothing,
> Not paying him his wages.
> . . .
> As for you, your looking and thinking
> Are concerned solely for what can be gained by violence;
> For shedding innocent blood,
> And committing oppression and violence.
> Therefore thus says the Lord regarding Jehoiakim
> . . .
> An ass's burial he'll have--
> Be dragged off and abandoned[2] beyond Jerusalem's gates.
>   (22:13; 17-18a, 19)

What Jehoiakim has done, the law prohibits (cp. Lev. 19:13 and Deut. 24:14-15; Ex. 23:7 and Deut. 27:25). His just "reward" will be "no burial."

Also instructive of the conjunction of an Ac. of behavior contrary to apodictic law with an AD whose content

---

are indicated on pp. 57-58.

[1]For the treaty-curse parallel and Hillers' discussion, see fn. 2, pp. 93-94, above.

[2]That השליך can convey "abandonment" has been shown by Morton Cogan in "A Technical Term for Exposure," *JNES*, 27

parallels treaty-curses is Mic. 6:10-15. Micah's accusation

begins with a question:

> Can I forget[1] treasures gained by wickedness in[2] the
>   house of the wicked
> And an accursed scant ephah?
> Can I regard as pure (those) with wicked scales
> And deceptive weights?
> The rich (of the city) are full of violence;
> Its inhabitants lie,
> Their tongue is deceitful in their mouth.
>   (6:10-12)

Such dishonesty in trade is contrary to what is enjoined by

apodictic law. Dishonest dealing is prohibited in Deut. 25:

13-15 and Lev. 19:35, while honesty is commended in Lev. 19:

36. The fruit of this dishonesty, declares Micah, will be

disaster, the content of which will include:

> As for you, you'll eat, but not be sated,
>
> . . .
> Though you'll overtake (prey), you'll not secure (it),
> And what you do secure I'll put to the sword.[3]
> You'll sow, but not reap;
> Tread olives, but not anoint with oil;

(1968), pp. 133-35. When the parallel to the "no burial"
curse is seen, the rendering "abandoned," or even "exposed,"
becomes apparent.

[1]Reading הַאֶשֶּׁה, from נשׁה , for האשׁ . Cp. J. M. P. Smith
A Critical and Exegetical Commentary on the Books of Micah,
Zephaniah and Nahum (New York: Charles Scribner's Sons,
1911), p. 130.

[2]For the use of the accusative, rather than "the
natural construction with ב," to express place, see G-K,
par. 118g.

[3]Verse 14b is difficult. We follow Hillers (Treaty-
Curses, p. 29) in taking "prey" as the understood object of
תסג. We understand תסג as a hiphil, from נשׂג.

And must, but you'll not drink wine.
                    (6:14-15)

What is striking is not the particular items which will
constitute the disaster, but the tone of futility which per-
vades the announcement. It is this tone which is typical of
some treaty-curses, leading Hillers to designate them "futility curses."[1]

   "Futility" is also the keynote of the disaster which
Amos announces for those whom he accuses in 5:11:

   Therefore because you trample on the poor,
   Taking from him exaction of corn,
   You may have built houses of hewn stone,
   But you'll not dwell in them;
   Planted delightful vineyards,
   But you'll not drink their wine.

The law forbids oppression of the poor (Ex. 22:20-21: Lev.
19:13a; Deut. 24:14);[2] therefore, their exploitation will
produce--nothing! Now focus on the words which express the
disaster; how closely they echo what is, in Deut. 28:30,
curse:[3]

---

[1]Ibid., pp. 28-29.

[2]Beyond the general indictment of oppression of the
poor, the relationship of 5:11a to apodictic law has been
considered by Bach ("Gottesrecht," p. 26). He sees the issue
as the taking of "Schuldzinsen," which is forbidden according
to Ex. 22:24 (cp. Lev. 25:36-37; Deut. 23:20). Cp., also,
Ernst Würthwein, "Amos-Studien," ZAW, 62 (1950), p. 46.

[3]So Hillers, Treaty-Curses, p. 29: "Amos 5:11 echoes
the Deuteronomy curse . . . ." A form-critical study of Deut.
28:30-31 leads Hillers to conclude "that the Deuteronomist
was . . . using older poetic materials" (pp. 35-37).

. . .
A house you'll build,
But dwell there never;
A vineyard plant,
But not enjoy it ever.

We have seen it in Jeremiah, in Micah, and now, in
Amos: an Ac. of behavior contrary to apodictic law, followed
by an AD whose similarity to treaty-curses is apparent. The
question must now be raised: Is this conjunction in the
passages we have considered--which is present, also, in other
passages referred to in footnote 2, pp. 93-94, above--mere
chance; or, is it possible that, for the prophets, the
effecting of a treaty-curse is the proper consequence of the
transgression of law because, for them, the law was part of
the covenant? The possibility of an affirmative answer to
this question would be furthered if we could affirm, as a
probability, that the prophets were aware of the treaty-association of these curses.

That one prophet was so aware is, indeed, probable. In
our study of Jer. 34:8-20 (pp. 66-72, above), we noted that
the prophet accused king and people of breaking a covenant by
which they had bound themselves to release their Hebrew
slaves (p. 72, above). Sheldon Blank has recovered by inference the ceremony by which that covenant had been sealed:

> They "cut" a covenant. A calf was led in and slaugh-
> tered, butchered, and divided down the middle. One
> half was laid over against the other with a passage
> between them . . . and then the covenanters walked
> the blood-sprinkled path between the pieces. Prob-
> ably, too, the agreement was read aloud; and whether

102

he spoke it or not each participant knew as he walked
that path that <u>he took on himself a conditional curse</u>.
If he failed to carry out his undertaking, in this
grisly fashion he, too, would be butchered.[1]

The underlined portion of the above quotation becomes significant when we notice how, having made the accusation of
covenant-breaking (vs. 16), Jeremiah begins his announcement
of its consequences:

> . . . I will make the men who transgressed my cove-
> nant . . . like the calf which they cut in two and
> passed between its parts . . .
> (34:18)

If Blank is correct about the covenant ceremony--that each
participant took upon himself a conditional curse--then the
propriety of the AD becomes manifest: <u>the punishment for
breach of covenant is to be activation of the covenant curse</u>.

That Jeremiah indeed saw it this way--covenant-breaking
elicits effected covenant curse(s)--receives corroborative
evidence from the continuation of the AD begun in verse 18.
As if death were not enough!

> . . . their corpses shall serve as food for the car-
> rion birds and wild beasts (34:20).

That this announcement of "no burial" has treaty-curse parallels has already been indicated in our discussion of 7:30-
34 (p. 96, above), where it also occurs.

---

[1] <u>Jeremiah</u>, p. 48. The form of this conditional curse
may be inferred from 34:20: e.g., "May I be made like the
calf . . ." The "simile curse" is one of the major treaty-
curse forms, and receives extended treatment by Hillers
(<u>Ibid</u>., pp. 18-26).

We are faced, then, in this passage, with a conjunction
of covenant-breaking with an activation of treaty-curses so
apparent, that it is difficult to escape the conviction that
Jeremiah, at least, knew a treaty-curse when he used one.

The case for a similar awareness on the part of the
eighth-century prophets whom we have been considering is not
so clear. It is enough for us here to have noted that their
words contain treaty-curse parallels. When we have inquired
whether other covenant elements can be observed in their
message, we will be better placed to make such a declaration.[1]

Before taking leave of the view that the prophets were
aware of the treaty-association of these curse-parallels
which appear in their message, we must meet a possible
objection. It is a point which has already engaged Hillers
in his book, Covenant: The History of a Biblical Idea.
Noting that a curse in a ninth-century Assyrian treaty which
has parallels in the prophets also appears in the Code of
Hammurapi, in the Baal epic from Ugarit, "and on the

---

[1]Hillers (Ibid.) assumes that they were so aware, and
makes his case on pp. 83-84. James L. Mays in Amos: A
Commentary (Philadelphia: The Westminster Press, 1969),
p. 94, states quite baldly that Amos was conscious of the
futility curse association of his announcement of disaster
in 5:11: "When Amos uses these formulations he is saying in
effect that Yahweh will invoke the sanctions of his covenant
with Israel against these perverters of Israel's social
order."

sarcophagus of King Ahiram of Byblos, warning away tomb rob-
bers," he is led to ask:

> Assuming that we might find the same thing to be true
> if we had fuller evidence about other curses (i.e., that
> they were used in non-treaty as well as treaty contexts),
> is there any reason for singling out the covenant or
> treaty as what was in the prophets' minds when they used
> such imagery?[1]

We are one with him in his answer:

> . . . yes, not because of the verbal parallels and the
> parallels in imagery in themselves, but because <u>there
> is such a similarity in function</u>. These threats are
> meant to work in the same way in the treaties, or
> biblical covenant-reports, and in the prophets. The
> same conceptual framework appears in each, but the
> prophets appear at a later stage, after the treaty is
> already broken. It is not just that a treaty says the
> gods will send wild animals and that the prophets say
> that Yahweh will do so, but that in the treaty the curse
> is invoked as the consequence for rebellion and that the
> prophetic doom is announced for the same reason--as the
> consequence of rebellion. The significant thing is that
> Jeremiah says "<u>Therefore</u> a lion from the forest shall
> smite them." We need an adequate explanation for this
> "therefore." . . . Only if we presuppose a relation
> binding Israel to God on pain of curses do the prophets
> seem logical.[2]

If Hillers is correct that the way the prophets use the

"verbal parallels and the parallels in imagery" indicates

that they were conscious of the treaty-association of the

curses, and since, as we have seen, these parallels form in

certain Prophetic Judgment-Speeches the content of the

---

[1]<u>Covenant</u>, p. 138. The explanatory words in parentheses are mine.

[2]<u>Ibid.</u>, pp. 138-39. The first underlining in the
quotation is ours, while Hillers emphasizes the word
"therefore."

punishment announced for behavior contrary to apodictic law,
our hypothesis that, for the prophets, the law was part of a
covenant whose form was that of a treaty continues to be
viable. A further direction for the pursuit of this thesis
is provided by the above quotation from Hillers. The suggestive words are: ". . . the prophetic doom is announced
. . . as the consequence of rebellion."

The Hebrew word פשע indicates an action which violates a treaty relationship. In the prophets, the content of פשע is often behavior contrary to apodictic law

The word "rebellion" is a loaded word for Hillers.
Witness his comment on his translation of the word פשע in
Jer. 2:8:

> The verb I have translated as "rebel" is originally
> a political term, and its use in the religious vo-
> cabulary is rooted in the political metaphor at the
> bottom of so much of the religion.[1]

Michael Fishbane, in his study of "The Treaty Background of Amos 1:11 and Related Matters," calls attention to
פשע as one example of "treaty expressions in the oracle
strophes of 1:1-2:16," and, at the same time, makes reference
to other biblical occurrences:

> The lead-verb, פשע , is a Begründung in these oracles
> and means "break a treaty," "rebel," both in context
> (I Kings 12:19; II Kings 3:7; 8:20,22 par. II Chron.
> 21:8, 10), and in parallelism (Is. 59:13; Ezek. 20:38;

---

[1] *Ibid.*, p. 130.

106

Hos. 8:1; Lam. 3:42).[1]

A reading of the examples cited by Fishbane from the
historical books suggests a certain framework in which פשע
is to be understood.

1.   פשע assumes a prior relationship between two peoples,
wherein the one who "rebels" has an inferior status to the
other. (E.g., Edom is a vassal of Judah. Cp. I Kings 22:47;
II Kings 3:9, where the king of Edom goes with Jehoshaphat to
aid Jehoram when Mesha "rebels"; and II Kings 8:20, 22, where
the phrase   מתחת יד־יהודה describes the subsidiary position
of Edom to Judah.)

2.   The inferior party "rebels" (פשע) against the superior
(II Kings 8:20, 22), leading to

3.   punitive action on the part of the superior against
the inferior (I Kings 12:21; II Kings 3:7; 8:21).

        In the prophets to whom we have directed our attention,
the second and third parts of this פשע framework of the historical books are clearly present: Israel "rebels," and God
punishes. Amos 2:6-16 is the locus classicus; verses 6a
and 13 being sufficient to illustrate the point:[2]

---

[1]Op. cit., p. 317.

[2]Other passages which state that Israel's "rebellions"
will incur divine punishment are Amos 5:12-13, 16-17; Mic. 1:
5-7; Jer. 5:6. In the Micah passage, God is agent as well as
author of the punitive action (see p. 82, above, for this
distinction).
We do not wish to engage in a discussion of the relationship

For Israel's three rebellions (פשעי ישראל) . . .

I'm going to cause a tottering under you,
As a cart filled with grain might totter.

At this point, we intend to take a close look at the second

element of the פשע framework: Israel "rebels." Let us see

how prophets answer the question: Of what does Israel's פשע

consist?

Israel's פשע according to Amos.

For Israel's three rebellions,
Yes--for four--I'll not be reconciled with him.[1]
Because they sell the innocent for (owing) "pocket
    change,"
The needy, for a "mere pittance."[2]

---

of Yahweh to other nations in Amos. They too, of course,
"rebel" (cp. 1:3, 6, etc.); and, in 9:7, God declares that
his activity on Israel's behalf at the Exodus did not differ
in kind from that with other nations. On the other hand, 3:2
implies a special relationship, as well as stating Israel's
special culpability. On 3:2a, see Herbert B. Huffmon, "The
Treaty Background of the Hebrew Yada," BASOR, 181 (February,
1966), pp. 31-37.

[1]For the hiphil of שוב to express "be reconciled
with"; cp. Jer. 15:19; 31:18.

[2]Amos' indictment is for slavery for debt (see fn. 4, p.
108, below). William Rainey Harper, A Critical and Exegetical
Commentary on Amos and Hosea (New York: Charles Scribner's
Sons, 1910), p. 49, suggests that "the phrase for a pair of
shoes seems to be a proverbial expression designating something of the lowest value." We therefore render the phrase
colloquially. We impute a similar connotation to בכסף in
the first colon, and also render it by a colloquialism. An
alternative interpretation of בעבור נעלים has been proposed
by E. A. Speiser, "Of Shoes and Shekels," BASOR, 77 (February, 1940), pp. 15-20. He points out that two documents
from Nuzi ". . . mention shoes not as items in the local
economy but as legal symbols" (p. 17). In these documents, a
ceremonial transfer of shoes serves to validate an otherwise
illegal transaction. Speiser therefore understands Amos to

They crush the poor as regards the head,[1]
Deprive the afflicted of due process.[2]
A man and his father go to the same maiden,
With the result that my name is profaned.
They recline on garments taken in pledge
Beside every altar;
They drink wine taken in payment of fines
In the house of their God (2:6-8).

Amos here give us a catalogue of "rebellions"; 1) im-
posing debt-servitude; 2) oppression of the poor; 3) perversion of justice; 4) father and son having intercourse with
the same girl;[3] 5) contumelious contumacy. Amos calls them
"rebellions," but they are also something else--actions contrary to apodictic law. Oppression is forbidden in Ex. 22:
20-21 and Lev. 19:13a. Perversion of justice is condemned
in Ex. 23:1-3 and Deut. 16:19. While apodictic law does not
expressly forbid father and son having intercourse with the

---

be alluding to ". . . a proverbial saying which refers to the
oppression of the poor by means which may be legal but do not
conform to the spirit of the law" (p. 18).

[1]The א in השאפים (2:7) is to be understood as a mater
lectionis; the root is שוף. We have omitted על-עפר-ארץ as
a gloss.

[2]For the rendering of דרך as "due process" (2:7), cp.
Victor Maag, Text, Wortschatz und Begriffswelt des Buches
Amos (Leiden: E. J. Brill, 1951), p. 142.

[3]That it is this, and not intercourse with a cult
prostitute, which Amos is indicting in 2:7b is argued by
Bach ("Gottesrecht," pp. 30-31). If intercourse with a cult
prostitute were Amos' accusation, says Bach, "Denn für diese
steht ja ein terminus technicus zur Verfügung . . ." (p. 30).
Further, it is really the second colon of 2:7b "das allein
diese Deutung allenfalls nahelegen könnte, . . . (but it) ist
wahrscheinlich nicht ursprünglich."

same girl, Bach's detailed treatment of 2:7b certainly indicates that such behavior would have been contrary to its
spirit.[1] The precise nature of the "contumacy(ies)" of which
Amos accuses his people in verse 8 in elusive. In 8a, he
seems to imply the disregard of the limitation which Ex. 22:
25 sets on pledged garments.[2] As for 8b: if William Rainey
Harper was correct that the issue was the source of the wine
("wine purchased by money received through unjust judgment");
then, this would be a further case (cp. vs. 7a) of perversion
of justice.[3] Of course, in verse 8, the issue is not only
the what, but also the where. They do these things "beside
every altar . . . in the house of their God"; that is, their
culpability is compounded by hubris--their behavior not only
contumacious, but contumelious. Finally, while the indictment of servitude for debt (6b) lacks a specific parallel,
Bach finds it to be against the tenor of apodictic law:

> So lässt sich . . . nur sagen, dass der Vorwurf des
> Amos sich mit einer der Grundtendenzen des apodik-
> tischen Rechts deckt (die Freiheit auch des letzten
> Israeliten zu sichern und zu wahren), ohne dass wir
> mit Sicherheit den Satz anzugeben vermöchten, auf
> den Amos sich berufen haben mag.[4]

---

[1]Ibid., pp. 32-33.

[2]Cp. Mays, Amos, p. 47. For Ex. 22:25 as having its
origin in apodictic law, see fn. 3, p. 65, above.

[3]Amos and Hosea, p. 50.

[4]"Gottesrecht," p. 29. That 2:6b is an indictment of
debt-servitude has been maintained by Harper (Ibid., p. 49)

In 5:12, Amos again gives פשע content:

Indeed, I know that your rebellions are many,
Your sins manifold--
Who are adversaries of the innocent, accept bribes,
And thrust aside the needy in the gate.

Here, once again, the "rebellions" consist of activities
designed to thwart justice; yet, it is justice which the
apodictic laws of Ex. 23:1-3 and Deut. 16:19 seek to uphold.

In 4:4, Israel's ritual practices are designated as
פשע by Amos. What is it about the cult that causes Amos to
label it thus? In large measure, cult is פשע for Amos because, for Israel, the fulfilling of the demands of cult has
displaced the fulfilling of the demands of God. Her whole
assumption is false. Cult is what Israel "loves to do"; not
what God wants her to do (4:5). Instead of devoting herself
to festivals which God "hates" (5:21), she should . . .

Let justice roll on as waters,
Righteousness as a perennial stream (5:24).

"Justice" and "righteousness" are antonyms for the social
injustices Amos everywhere denounces.[1] Because the cult
fosters these injustices by substituting a synthetic demand
of God for his real demand, it has become פשע along with the

---

as well as Bach.

[1]Mays discusses משפט and צדק in Amos on pp. 91-93 of
his commentary (op. cit.). Of 5:7 and 6:12b which indict
Israel for perversion of משפט and צדק, Mays says: "These
formulations could stand as summations for all of Amos' com-
plaints against Israel's social order" (p. 92).

injustices it has fostered. Further, some of the proceeds
from these social injustices may have been used in the performance of the cult. As we have seen, 2:8 suggests that the
garments on which the cultic participants reclined, and perhaps also the wine they drank, were fruits of the disregard
of certain requirements of apodictic law (cp. p. 109, above).
If so, Israel's cult would deserve the designation פשע , not
only because it fostered a disregard of the demands of God,
but because it benefited directly from that disregard.

פשע in Micah.

Of the five verses where a form of פשע occurs, we omit
1:13 from consideration.[1] In the remaining cases, it parallels a form of חטא three times (1:5; 3:8; 6:7) and עון once
(7:18). Thus, in Micah, פשע has a negative connotation and
is a comprehensive designation for those things that (Israel)
has done which: are deserving of punishment (1:5), which the
prophet is commissioned to "declare" to his people (3:8),
which need atonement (6:7), and which God, in his compassion,
forgives (7:18). For the denotation of פשע, only 1:5, 3:8,
and 6:7 are suggestive. However, because of the difficulty
in delimiting the oracle of which 1:5 is a part, and because

_____

[1]The relevant portions of 1:13 may be secondary (cp.
Beyerlin, Kulttraditionen, pp. 13-14); and, in any case, we
learn nothing about the content of Israel's "rebellions"--
only that Lachish is similarly afflicted. 7:18 is probably
also secondary, though we include it because it is, at least,
comprehensible, whereas 1:13 is not.

the genuineness of 1:5c and 1:7 is a matter of considerable debate, the content of the "rebellion"/"sins" of 1:5 does not admit of being established with any certainty.[1] With respect to 3:8, provided that we are granted one assumption, it can furnish a clue to Micah's understanding of פשע. That assumption is: Micah carried out the commission of which he there speaks:

> But as for me, I am filled with power,
> With the spirit of the Lord,
> And with justice and might,
> To declare to Jacob his rebellion (פשעו),
> To Israel his sin.

Granted this assumption, we need only look at the content of Micah's accusations to learn in what Israel's פשע consists. As we have previously noted (p. 65, above), this has been done by Walter Beyerlin, who has shown that the behavior indicted by Micah is, again and again, to be seen in opposition to apodictic law.[2] It is, then, such behavior which constitutes, for Micah, Israel's "rebellion." The content of the פשע of 6:7 must be inferred from context. Our study of 6:1-8 (pp. 131-145, below) will show that that for which Israel admits culpability in 6:7 (פשעי) is commensurate with

---

[1]For an argument that 1:5c and 1:7 are secondary, see Beyerlin, Ibid., pp. 13-14. For the delimitation of the oracle, see the various commentaries as well as the standard Old Testament introductions. If 1:7 is original and does belong with 1:5, then idolatry would be a constituent of פשע for Micah.

[2]Ibid., pp. 50-64.

that which Micah indicts in fulfillment of his commission

recorded in 3:8.

פשע in Isaiah.

פשע appears only in 1:2 among the material to be attributed to Isaiah of Jerusalem.[1] The verse is part of a

"covenant lawsuit" (1:2-3, 10-20) which will be discussed in

detail below (pp. 127-131). It will there be seen that that

for which Israel is indicted--that which constitutes her פשע

--is her participation in social injustice, the doing of cer-

tain things which, according to apodictic law, she ought not

to have done.

פשע in Jeremiah.

פשע occurs five times in Jeremiah. Of these, 33:8 may

be omitted from consideration. It is part of a passage which

appears to be secondary, and, in any case, gives פשע no def-

inite content.[2] Of the remaining occurrences, 2:29 (29-32),

3:13, and 5:6 clearly associate פשע with apostasy. Only 2:8

presents difficulty:

---

[1]1:28 is secondary. Cp. Bernhard Duhm, Das Buch
Jesaia, GHAT (Göttingen: Vandenhoeck & Ruprecht, 1914), pp.
12-13; R. B. Y. Scott, The Book of Isaiah: Chapters 1-39,
IB, Vol. V, p. 179. If our concern were to study "rebellion," rather than the word פשע we would have to take
account, particularly in Isaiah, of the roots מרה (cp. 30:9)
and סרר (cp. 30:1).

[2]Cp. Volz, Jeremia, p. 310.

> The priests did not say, "Where is the Lord?"
> Those who handle the law did not know me.
> The רעים rebelled against me;
> The prophets prophesied by Baal,
> Pursued the profitless.

Our problem is, who did what; i.e., who are the רעים, and what was their "rebellion." The answer of the commentators is unanimous; the רעים are the political leaders, and their "rebellion" was . . .(?):[1] While the inclination to follow their lead is strong (to say that we do not know in what their "rebellion" consisted), we assert that the question can be answered, as soon as it is seen that the רעים are not (in 2:8) political leaders, but prophets: their "rebellion" is that they "prophesied by Baal" (i.e., apostasy). Our argument is brief:

1. Some commentators see the first two cola as referring to a single group; the priests.[2] If so, why cannot the third and fourth cola, similarly, refer to a single group; the prophets?

2. In 17:16, the prophet says: "I did not try to escape

---

[1]E.g., Bright, _Jeremiah_, p. 15; Peake, _Jeremiah_ I, p. 91; Rudolph, _Jeremia_, p. 12; Volz, _Jeremia_, p. 19.

[2]E.g., Rudolph, _Jeremia_, p. 12. Prescott H. Williams discusses the question of whether the תפשי התורה are the priests or a separate class of religious functionaries in his "The Fatal and Foolish Exchange: Living Water for 'Nothings,'" _Austin Seminary Bulletin_, LXXXI (September, 1965), pp. 27-30. Williams concludes on the basis of the way in which various groups of leaders are referred to elsewhere in Jer. 1-25 that the phrase does not have in mind a separate class of priests (p. 30).

from being your shepherd" (מרעה אחריך).[1] If Jeremiah can
call himself a רעה, then the רעים of 2:8 can be prophets.
3. As we shall see later, "not knowing" (of which the
priests are accused) is analogous to, if not synonymous with,
"rebelling." Thus, in the first colon of 2:8, the behavior
of the priests is specified (not saying, "Where is the
Lord?"), while in the second, it is described as "not knowing
me." In the third colon, the behavior of the prophets (רעים)
is given a general designation ("they rebelled"), while in
the fourth, it is given specific content (they "prophesied by
Baal").

Therefore, we understand the point of 2:8 to be: those
who had the special task of preventing apostasy (priests and
prophets) were themselves apostate; thereby affording no help
to an apostate people. Thus, in 2:8 also, the content of
פשע is apostasy.

פשע: Summary and Conclusion.

We have been asking of our prophets: Of what does
Israel's פשע consist? Our search has gleaned the following:
1. For Amos, פשע has a specific content: certain precise
items of social behavior which contravene apodictic law.
Israel's cult is also פשע, for it fosters this behavior and
benefits from it.

---

[1]The מ of מרעה has a privative force.

2. For Micah, פשע was to be the butt of his message (3:8).
Central to his actual preaching were accusations of behavior
which apodictic law opposes. We may take it then that, for
Micah, פשע was a general term for the totality of "no-no's"
perpetrated by Israel.

3. Isaiah uses the word פשע only in the "covenant lawsuit"
of 1:2-3, 10-20. It there summarizes Yahweh's case against
Israel. The substance of Yahweh's case is that Israel has
done certain things which, as will be shown below (pp. 127-
131), are forbidden by apodictic law.

4. In Jeremiah, פשע designates apostasy, the "rebellion" par
excellence. To be sure, פשע in Jeremiah contravenes apodictic
law, just as do the "rebellions" which Amos censures; and,
Jeremiah has not lost sight of this fact (cp. 7:9, where
apostasy is cited with other transgressions of apodictic law).
However, in Jeremiah, the "feel" is different. When Amos
accuses Israel of "rebellions," it is like an indictment read
in court; when one reads Jeremiah's recounting of his people's
apostasy, it is like reading the report of a murder in a
newspaper--the horror of the thing done tends to submerge the
fact that it is a crime.

The Hebrew word פשע is a treaty expression which
signifies that a treaty has been violated. One constituent
of פשע for the prophets is behavior contrary to apodictic
law. Thus we have additional evidence that, for the prophets,

117

the law was part of the covenant.

The Hebrew word ידע has a treaty background. This covenant
reference of ידע appears to be present in some prophetic
passages. In these same passages, ידע often entails conduct
similar to that enjoined by apodictic law

Herbert B. Huffmon has shown that, in the ancient Near
Eastern treaty materials, "know" appears as a terminus technicus with two senses: to recognize the legitimacy of a
suzerain or vassal, and to recognize treaty stipulations as
binding.[1] Huffmon has noticed two places in the prophets
where ידע conveys the idea of Yahweh's covenant recognition
of Israel (i.e., Yahweh's recognition of Israel as his legitimate vassal): Amos 3:2 and Hosea 13:5.[2] ידע is also found
in prophetic passages where the meaning "recognize as suzerain," or "recognize the authority of" is appropriate.
Huffmon views Jer. 2:8; 22:16; 24:7; 31:34 and a number of
passages from Hosea in this light.[3]

When one comes upon a new meaning for a word, it is
easy to get carried away--having seen its applicability some-
where, one is inclined to look for its applicability everywhere. Nevertheless, we would expand Huffmon's Jeremiah list

---

[1]"The Treaty Background of Hebrew Yada," BASOR, 181
(February, 1966), pp. 31-37. See also Huffmon and Simon B.
Parker, "A Further Note on the Treaty Background of Hebrew
Yada," BASOR, 184 (December, 1966), pp. 36-38.

[2]"Treaty Background," pp. 34-35.

[3]Ibid.. pp. 35-37.

to include 4:22; 9:2, 5, 23, where the recognition of Yahweh's suzerainty/authority also seem to be implied. Further,
we would also understand ידע in Isaiah 1:3 in this way. When
1:2-3 are taken together, the covenant imagery is unmistak-
able:

> Listen heaven! Pay attention earth!
> The Lord has spoken:
> "Splendid children I've raised,
> But they've rebelled (פשע) against me.
> An ox knows (ידע; i.e., recognizes the authority of)
>   its owner,
> And an ass its master's crib;
> But Israel does not know (ידע ; recognize its suze-
>   rain),
> My people does not understand."

1. We have already seen that פשע is a treaty word. (לא)
ידע in verse three is the equivalent of פשע in verse two.

2. Heaven and earth are invoked as covenant-witnesses in
the Hittite treaties and play a similar role here in a "covenant lawsuit."[1]

3. The relationship between Yahweh and Israel is characterized as a father-son relationship. The use of the father-
son analogy to express the covenant relationship between
Yahweh and Israel is characteristic of the Bible.[2]

---

[1]Herbert B. Huffmon, "Covenant Lawsuit," points out
that an appeal to natural elements is characteristic of the
covenant lawsuit. He argues that the reason for the appeal
to the natural elements is ". . . because they are witnesses
to the (prior) covenant" (p. 292).

[2]This is argued by Dennis J. McCarthy in "Notes on the
Love of God in Deuteronomy and the Father-Son Relationship
Between Yahweh and Israel," CBQ, XXVII (1965). pp. 144-47.

Finally, the treaty background of ידע is reflected in
Jer. 7:9; 19:4; 44:3, where ידע is used not with Yahweh as
object, but "other gods." It is stated that these "other
gods," the object of the people's apostasy, were not "known"
to them (or their fathers); i.e., were not recognized by them
as suzerain.

Thus there is in Jeremiah (and Hosea) a spate of passages where covenant recognition or its lack is connoted by
ידע. Amos and Isaiah have one verse each where ידע is so
used (Amos 3:2 and Is. 1:3). We must now inquire whether
this "knowing" is merely expressive of a relationship, or
whether there is content to it as well.

We have already had occasion to look at a part of the
Woe-Speech of Jer. 22:13-19 (see pp. 62 and 98, above). In
the verses we have examined, the prophet accuses Jehoiakim
of behavior contrary to apodictic law (vss. 13 and 17) and
announces as judgment that the king's lot will be "no burial"
(vs. 19). As if this were not enough, Jehoiakim must suffer
the prophet's comparing him with his illustrious father:

> Now your father, didn't he . . .
> Practice justice and righteousness . . . ?
> Take up the cause of the poor and needy . . .
> Isn't this knowledge of me?--it is the Lord speaking.
> (22:15b-16)

"Knowledge of God," recognizing Yahweh's suzerainty, is

See also, McCarthy, "Covenant in the Old Testament," _ibid._,
pp. 234-35.

demonstrated in the realm of conduct. It means performing
"justice and righteousness," one example of which is--for a
king--espousing "the cause of the poor and needy." Earlier
in the same chapter Jeremiah states more precisely what the
royal performance of "justice and righteousness" entails:[1]

> . . . deliver the robbed from the power of the op-
> pressor, maltreat neither resident alien, orphan,
> nor widow, commit no violence, shed no innocent
> blood in this place (22:3).

Jeremiah is not squeamish about indicting kings; but, at the
same time, he has a program--a royal platform--of what the
good king should do. And, just as he accused Jehoiakim of
behavior contrary to apodictic law, so he commends Josiah
for--and enjoins upon all kings--practicing "justice and
righteousness," specific details of which correspond closely
to apodictic law; for, again and again, apodictic law is
concerned with protecting the weak from oppression (e.g., Ex.
22:20-21; Lev. 19:13a; Deut. 27:19). Such things Josiah did,
and the doing was accounted to him as "knowledge of God."

But, a style of life which exhibits "knowledge of God"
is, according to Jeremiah, incumbent upon not just king, but
people as well. Unfortunately, it is just the opposite which
Jeremiah witnesses:

> . . . they're all adulterers, a band of dissemblers.

---

[1]We understand the waw which precedes הצילו as an
explicative waw, to be translated "namely," or "that is."

They bend their tongue like a bow.[1]
Falsehood and not faithfulness prevails in the land.[2]
For from evil to evil they've gone,
While me they don't know--it is the Lord speaking.
Each must beware of his fellow
And you can't even trust a brother,
For every brother's a proverbial Jacob
And every friend goes about telling tales.
They deceive one another
And don't speak truth.
They have taught their tongue to speak falsehood;
They have acted perversely, they cannot do otherwise.[3]
Oppression upon oppression, deceit upon deceit;
They have refused to know me--it is the Lord
    speaking (9:1-5).

Thus Jeremiah describes the disintegration of society,
the dissolution of community. This is a freer composition
than the "temple sermon" of chapter 7, but this indictment
also has its echoes of apodictic law:

You shall not commit adultery (Ex. 20:14).

You shall not lie[4] (Lev. 19:11c).

You shall not go about as a talebearer among your
    people (Lev. 19:16a).

---

[1]Reading וידרכו as kal with pause after קשתם in
vs. 2a.

[2]Beginning vs. 2b with שקר; reading אמונה for
לאמונה ; reading גבר for גברו .

[3]Reading the end of vs. 4 and the beginning of vs. 5 as
follows: הֶעֱוּי נלאוּ שָׁב : אַף .

[4]The root of the verb we have translated "lie" is שקר .
The noun we have translated "falsehood" in Jer. 9:2, 4, is
שֶׁקֶר .

122

In Jeremiah, "knowing God" has a content.[1] This "content" is a type of conduct having features which are also stressed by apodictic law. Conversely, a people whose life displays those things which apodictic law forbids are said to not "know" God.

Since לא ידע in Isaiah 1:3 is parallel to פשע in 1:2, what we have said of the content of פשע (p. 113, above) may be applied to לא ידע. If so, it is Israel's activities contrary to certain requirements of apodictic law that enables Isaiah to say of her, "Israel does not know."

In Amos 3:2, what is at issue is not what it means for a people to "know" God (i.e., recognize his suzerainty in a covenant relationship), but what it means for God to "know" a people (i.e., recognize them as his legitimate vassal):

> You alone do I know
> Of all the families of the earth;
> Therefore I will punish you
> For all your iniquities.

When God recognizes a people by covenant, he may expect certain things of them. When these obligations are not fulfilled (i.e., when his people commits "iniquities"), he will punish. What are these "iniquities" whose commission by

---

[1]For an admirable discussion of "knowledge of God" in Jeremiah, see Blank, _Jeremiah_, pp. 184-88. We have limited our own search for the content of ידע in Jeremiah to 1) those passages where God (as opposed to e.g., דרך יהוה or משפט יהוה) is the object of ידע ; and 2) those passages where a definitive content for ידע can be gleaned from the context (as opposed to, e.g., 4:22).

123

Israel elicits divine punishment?

Assuming that, in 3:1-2, we are dealing with an independent oracle, then James L. Mays has fixed both the problem and its solution:

> What these iniquities are is not said here. For the particulars of Amos' indictment of Israel one has merely to listen to the indictments which are the basis of most of his announcements of judgment.[1]

Among Israel's "iniquities," then, would be her various transgressions of apodictic law and the cult which both fosters and benefits from these transgressions (cp. pp. 107-111, above).

In three of the prophets with whom we are concerned we have noted a special use of the Hebrew word ידע . It is found with this special meaning particularly in Jeremiah, but also in Isaiah 1:3 and Amos 3:2. On the one side, ידע points to the covenant between Yahweh and Israel and means "recognize as suzerain/vassal by covenant." On the other side, to "know" or "be known" by God demands a certain conduct, a conduct which, as we have seen, apodictic law also enjoins. Further, Amos 3:2 declares that God will punish his vassal, Israel, for doing things which apodictic law forbids. We

---

[1]Amos, p. 58. In treating 3:1-2 as an originally independent saying, we follow the majority of scholars. Maag (Amos, p. 13), following Budde, understands 3:1-2 as the conclusion of 1:3-2:16. Israel's "iniquities" would then be the פשעים enumerated in 2:6 ff. which, as we have shown above (pp. 107-110), were in violation of several apodictic laws.

might encapsulate this part of the message of these prophets
in this way: "If you would know God (or be known by him),
observe his laws." Thus does our study of another treaty
expression further our hypothesis that, for the prophets, the
law was part of the covenant.

Contemporary scholarship has delineated the "covenant lawsuit" form. In the prophetic examples of this form, that
behavior for which Israel is indicted and which constitutes
breach of covenant is behavior which apodictic law forbids;
and/or, that which is demanded of the accused--that which can
prevent the dissolution of the covenant--is behavior consonant with apodictic law

In a 1959 article, "The Covenant Lawsuit in the Prophets," Herbert B. Huffmon distinguished two types of "lawsuit"
oracles in the Old Testament.[1] One type he declared to be
"connected with the divine council," while the other "is an
indictment of Israel for breach of covenant."[2] Characteristic of the "covenant lawsuit" is "an appeal to the natural
elements" (e.g., Is. 1:2; Mic. 6:2; Jer. 2:12) and an "historical prologue" (e.g., Is. 1:2; Mic. 6:4-5; Jer. 2:6-7),
features which are also characteristic of the Hittite treaties.[3] In the prophetic literature, Huffmon considers

---

[1]Op. cit., fn. 2, p. 83, above.

[2]Ibid., p. 295.

[3]Ibid., For the "appeal to natural elements" in the
Hittite treaties see ibid., p. 291 and Mendenhall, Law and
Covenant, p. 34. Huffmon also draws attention (p. 292) to
three prose passages in Deuteronomy (4:26; 30:19; 31:28)
where heaven and earth are invoked as covenant witnesses;

Is. 1:2-3 (1:2-20), Mic. 6:1-8, and Jer. 2:4-13 as conforming
to this pattern.

The most recent treatment of the "lawsuit" form is that
of Julien Harvey in Le Plaidoyer prophetique contre Israël
apres la rupture de l'alliance.[1] Though he would delimit the
Isaiah and Jeremiah passages differently (Is. 1:2-3, 10-20;
Jer. 2:4-13, 29), these three passages (which were, for
Huffmon, the only prophetic examples of the "covenant lawsuit" form) are considered by Harvey in his analysis of "Les
requisitoires complets dans l'A.T."[2]

Harvey finds five features to be constitutive of "les
requisitoires complets":[3]

1. The calling of heaven and earth as covenant-witnesses
    and summoning of the defendants.

2. Interrogation (addressed by the judge/plaintiff to the
    accused).

3. Indictment (usually in historical terms--the benefits of

---

i.e., in the Old Testament, itself, the appeal to heaven and
earth is connected with the covenant. For the "historical
prologue" of the Hittite treaties, see Mendenhall, ibid.,
pp. 32-33.

[1]Op. cit., fn. 2, p. 83, above.

[2]Ibid., pp. 31-56. The remaining examples of "les
requisitoires complets" are, according to Harvey, Deut. 32
and Psalm 50. These are also Huffmon's only non-prophetic
examples of covenant lawsuits.

[3]Ibid., pp. 54-55.

Yahweh being contrasted with the misdeeds of his people-
but often including a rejection of foreign gods and
sacrificial rites).

4. Declaration of the culpability of the people.

5. Condemnation (expressed in the form of threats) or
   Positive Decree (which states the new attitudes demanded
   by the plaintiff of the accused).

The fifth element is particularly significant because, de-
pending upon its content, the lawsuit is a "rîb absolu"
(Condemnation) or a "rîb mitigé" (Positive Decree). Let
us see how the various elements appear in our prophetic
passages:[1]

		Is. 1	Jer. 2	Mic. 6
1.	Calling of Witnesses and Defendants	2a, 10	4-5a, 12	2
2.	Interrogation	11-12	5b-6	3
3.	Historical Indictment	2b-3	7-11	4-5
	Rejection of Gods and Sacrifices	13-15b		6-8a

---

[1]Following the table of Harvey on p. 54, with the
exception of the underlined vss., Is. 1:2b-3. For Harvey,
these verses illustrate a separate element, "Déclaration de
la rectitude de Yahvé et accusation du peuple," which comes
between the Calling of Witnesses and the Interrogation. It
is the only example of this element in the three prophetic
passages, though it appears in Deut. 32:4-5 and Psalm 50:6-7
Formally, Harvey is correct; however, in the Isaiah passage
which otherwise lacks an Historical Indictment, these verses
function as one, in nuce, and so we place them there, in our
table. for this reason.

	Is. 1	Jer. 2	Mic. 6
4. Declaration of Culpability	15c	13, 29	
5. Condemnation		(14 ff.)	
Positive Decree	16-20		8b-c

Let us reiterate that these are "covenant lawsuits":
each has an appeal to natural elements (Is. 1:2a; Jer. 2:12;
Mic. 6:2a), and in each, the divine beneficence (in Jer. 2:6-
7 and Mic. 6:4-5 in terms of "Heilsgeschichte"; in Is. 1:2b
in terms of family history) is declared.

For what is the defendant indicted in these passages?
i.e., what has he done which constitutes breach of covenant?
In Jer. 2, the answer is clear: Israel has committed
apostasy. This is stated in question form in the Interrogation (Jer. 2:5b; cp. the "accusing question" of the PJS),
emphasized by explicit statement at the conclusion of the
Historical Indictment (2:11), and stated for a third time in
the Declaration of Culpability (2:13). The indictment for
apostasy is, according to Harvey, typical of the "rib absolu":

> Cependant la grande majorité des réquisitoires ne
> sont pas provoqués par des infractions à l'une ou
> l'autre des stipulations de l'alliance, mais par
> l'infraction collective contre le premier commande-
> ment, que nous distinguons ici de la "déclaration
> fondamentale" de l'alliance.[1]

For reasons which will become clear shortly, we will set out

---

[1] Ibid., p. 94.

the form and content of the indictment procedure according
to Jer. 2 using, however, our own words, and placing Harvey's
terms in parentheses:

The defendant is charged with apostasy (Interrogation).
5b-6.

The evidence establishes the defendant's apostasy
(Historical Indictment). 7-11.

The defendant is guilty of apostasy as charged (Declaration of Culpability). 13.

According to the Jeremiah passage, then, Israel, by her
apostasy, has broken the covenant. We need only note that
apostasy is forbidden by apodictic law (Ex. 20:3).

When we come to the question of that for which the
defendant is indicted in Is. 1:2-3, 10-20, we are faced
squarely by an issue which has continued to loose the
scholarly pen:[1] did Isaiah (or Amos, Hosea, or Jeremiah as
the case may be) really mean what he apparently says in 1:11-
15?--no sacrifices! (Let it immediately be said that sacrifices to Yahweh is the issue here, as opposed to, e.g., "le
réquisitoire complet" of Deut. 32:1-25, where, in vss. 16-17,
the defendant is indicted for sacrifices to other gods.) We
approach the problem by way of a consideration of the form
and content of the indictment procedure using, once again,

---

[1]For a bibliography of works dealing with the question
of the prophetic attitude toward the cult, see Clements,
Prophecy and Covenant, p. 95, fn. 2, or Harvey, Le Plaidoyer
prophétique, p. 97, fn. 4.

our own words, with Harvey's terms in parentheses:

> The defendant is charged with offering sacrifices (Interrogation). 11-12.
>
> God rejects the defendant's cultic activities (Rejection of Sacrifices). 13-15b.
>
> The defendant is guilty of having "hands filled with blood": (?) (Declaration of Culpability). 15c.

In Jer. 2 we met with the pattern: charged with apostasy; indicted for apostasy; guilty of apostasy--here we have: charged with offering sacrifices; rejection of cultic activities; guilty of having "hands filled with blood." That is, in Jer. 2, we met with an identity in content of the three formal elements; here, in Isaiah, we would expect, if not identity, at least consonance. And, in the first two elements in the Isaiah passage, we do have consonance, for both have to do with cultic activities (vss. 11-12 and 13-15b). What of the third element? What is the prophet declaring Israel to be guilty of when he says, "Your hands are full of blood"? It is not the blood of sacrifices; for, as is pointed out in Gesenius-Kautzsch, the singular, דם, would be required.[1] We would assert that it is the opposite of that for which the prophet pleads in vss. 16-17; i.e., it is the blood of injustice and oppression, the blood of the orphan and widow whose cause has no advocate.[2] Thus, we have

---

[1]G-K, 124n.

[2]Cp. Edward J. Kissane, The Book of Isaiah, Vol. I (Dublin: Richview Press for Browne and Nolan Limited, 1960),

the defendant being: charged with sacrifice; indicted for

cultic activities; declared guilty of violence!   Is this

sensible?   This sequence is very much like an incident from

my childhood.

I was helping mother with the dishes when father came

into the kitchen:

Father: "Why are you helping mother with the dishes?"
           (Interrogation)

Son: "I just thought I'd give her a hand."

Father: "Your help with the dishes doesn't matter."
           (Indictment: Rejection of Dish-doing)

Father: "You didn't spade the garden for her today."
           (Declaration of Culpability)

How similar to the apparent non-sequitur which we have found

in Isaiah!   Here, the defendant is: charged with helping

with the dishes; indicted for helping with the dishes; but,

guilty of not spading the garden.   The sequence becomes

sensible only when the information is supplied that when

---

p. 12:   ". . . their hands are <u>full</u> <u>of</u> <u>blood</u>, i.e. they are
the hands of men who have been guilty of violence and even
bloodshed."   The phrase gathers up in a vivid metaphor the
crimes which Isaiah denounces elsewhere.   The movement in
the mind of the prophet from the blood of sacrifices in vs.
11 to the blood of injustice in vs. 15 is captured by
Bernhard Duhm: "Wahrscheinlich haben die Angeredeten, die
eben opfern, wirkliches Blut an den Händen; dies Blut, an
sich schon Jahve zuwider v. 11, wird dem Redner durch eine
natürliche Ideenassoziation zu einem Sinnbild für all das
blutige Unrecht, das in Jerusalem geschieht, die Vergewaltig-
ung der Rechtspflege, die Unterdrückung der Schwachen, mögen
die Angeredeten dergleichen selber tun oder doch geschehen
lassen" (<u>Jesaia</u>, pp. 8-9).

father left for work that morning he instructed me to help
mother by spading the garden. That is, what would normally
have been praiseworthy had become indictable--in the context
of disobedience.

With respect to Is. 1, we would understand the dis-
parity of content of the Declaration of Culpability (15c)
with the content of the Interrogation (11-12) and Indictment
(13-15b) in a similar way: Israel's cultic activity has become indictable because of her disobedience. Just as in my
relationship with my family, when I had disobeyed (rupturing
the relationship thereby) my helping with the dishes became
unacceptable; so, in Israel's relationship with Yahweh, when
she disobeyed (rupturing the relationship thereby) her cultic
activities became unacceptable. Just so does Harvey explain
the presence of the rejection of cultic activities in the
"rib":

> . . . il ne faut pas faire dire à ces textes plus
> qu'ils n'entendent affirmer, à savoir que les com-
> pensations rituelles ne valent plus rien dans le
> moment présent. Or, ce moment présent où le rib
> est pronouncé, c'est celui où l'alliance, lien fon-
> damental et prérequis à tout culte, est rompue.[1]

So, for Isaiah, the covenant has been broken, making sacrifices unacceptable. What is it that Israel did which broke

---

[1]Op. cit., pp. 98-99. The other reason which Harvey
offers for the presence in the "rib" of references "à
l'inanité des compensations cultuelles" is "que la situation
vitale dans laquelle venait s'insérer le rib était liturgique
et comprenait un sacrifice . . ." (p. 98).

the covenant? If we are correct in our interpretation of רמים (15c), it was her complicity in injustice and oppression, her lack of concern for the orphan and widow--the doing of those things which, according to apodictic law, she ought not to have done (cp. Ex. 22:20-21; Deut. 24:17; 27:19).

Micah 6:1-8 is replete with problems for the inter- preter, beginning with the questions of genuineness and unity. In the last two decades, the pendulum of scholarly consensus has swung in favor of Micah's authorship.[1] Fohrer, however, has argued against its genuineness, not as had been the custom on the basis of the content of the passage, but primarily on the basis of his view of the growth of the prophetic books: since, in Fohrer's view, the prophetic books grew in accordance with an eschatological schema of disaster followed by deliverance, the promises of chapters 4- 5 must signal the end of the material to be attributed to Micah.[2] If, however, one thinks of chapters 4-5 as a unit-- either as a "collection of individual sayings of unknown

---

[1]E.g., Beyerlin, Kulttraditionen, p. 50, fn. 3; Eissfeldt, Introduction, p. 411; Lindblom, Prophecy, p. 251; Artur Weiser, Das Buch der zwolf Kleinen Propheten, I (Göttingen: Vandenhoeck & Ruprecht, 1949), pp. 203, 251.

[2]Fohrer's argument appears on p. 446 of his Introduction. For the standard arguments against Mican authorship see, e.g., Smith, op. cit., p. 124. Since these arguments have been refuted by the scholars mentioned in the previous fn. and others, we have chosen to concentrate on Fohrer's argument which is different in kind.

eschatological prophets of the postexilic period" (or of any
period or periods), or as an independent complex of tradi-
tion--then, an eschatological schema (i.e., first, all
Micah's threats were collected; then, promises were appended
thereto) need not be the only, or even the most logical,
explanation for the present position of these chapters.[1] The
position of the unit (4-5) can be explained, quite simply, by
the theme of its first verses (4:1-4), the exaltation of
Zion. The PJS of 3:9-12 which declares the degradation and
impending devastation of Zion needed an antidote, and this
was provided by the affixing thereto of chapters 4-5 which
began with a pericope which proclaimed Zion's coming glory.[2]
Thus we see in chapters 4-5 not the second half of an eschatological schema which marks the end of the genuinely Mican
material, but an interruption of Micah's oracles in order to
pay obeisance to a "proper" Zion theology. Therefore, we do
not accept Fohrer's argument from "the growth of the proph-
etical books," and retain 6:1-8 for Micah.[3]

---

[1]The words in quotation marks are from Fohrer, ibid.,
p. 446. Eduard Nielsen, Oral Tradition (London: SCM Press,
1961), pp. 79-93, deals with Micah 4-5 as a tradition-complex.

[2]Nielsen (ibid., pp. 91-92) also explains the position
of chs. 4-5 by the mention of Zion in 3:9-12 and 4:1-4.
Whether any or what parts of these chapters are to be attributed to Micah is not here our concern. We seek only to give
an alternative (to Fohrer's) reason for the position of these
chapters.

[3]Fohrer supports his argument for a post-exilic date by

With respect to the question of unity, we stand with
recent studies of the "rib-pattern" which treat the passage
as a unit.[1] We will rest our case on our ability to demonstrate that, when taken as a whole, 6:1-8 makes sense. We
will begin by setting out the relevant parts of the passage
in accordance with the elements delineated by Harvey.

Interrogation (6:3).
"My people, what have I done to you,
How have I exhausted your patience? Answer me.

Historical Indictment (6:4-5).
Indeed, I brought you up from the land of Egypt,
From the house of bondage I redeemed you.
I sent before you Moses,
Aaron and Miriam.
My people, remember, won't you, what Balak, the
    king of Moab, plotted,
And how Balaam, the son of Beor, answered him.
. . . from Shittim to Gilgal,
That you might acknowledge the righteous deeds
    of the Lord."

Rejection of Sacrifices, within which is included
the Declaration of Culpability in the form of the
people's confession of culpability (6:6-8a).[2]

---

noting the presence in 6:1-8 of "wisdom theology, with its
emphasis on the role of the individual . . ." (op. cit., p.
446). However, 6:8 may be understood as emanating from a
covenant milieu (see fn. 1, p. 138, below), and we
understand the community to be the addressee of the entire
unit (Harvey, Le Plaidoyer prophétique, p. 43, points out
that the singular collective persists throughout vss. 3-8).

[1]Harvey, ibid., pp. 42-45; Huffmon, "Covenant Lawsuit,"
pp. 286-87.

[2]Cp. Harvey, ibid., p. 45: "On remarquera une modification importante: la déclaration de culpabilité, qui
termine régulièrement le réquisitoire, est ici inclue dans
l'aveu de culpabilité du peuple ('. . . pour ma rébellion . .
pour mon péché . . .')."

"With what shall I come before the Lord,
Bow myself to God on high?
Shall I come before him with burnt offerings,
With yearling calves?
Would the Lord accept with favor thousands of rams,
Myriads of streams of oil?
Shall I give my first born for my rebellion,
The fruit of my body for my sin?"
"It has been declared to you, man, what is good.

Positive Decree (6:8b-c).
And what does the Lord require of you
Except your doing justice, loving faithfulness,
And walking humbly with your God?"

Let us ask of these verses the same questions we asked

of the Jeremiah and Isaiah passages:

With what is the defendant charged?

For what is he indicted?

Of what is he declared guilty?

Hillers and Westermann hold that the defendant, Israel,[1] is

charged/indicted for apostasy.[2] Such a charge would be

_____

[1]Childs (Memory and Tradition, p. 56) and Gerhard von
Rad, Old Testament Theology, Vol. II, trans. by D. M. G.
Stalker (New York: Harper & Row, 1965), p. 38, fn. 10, see
Yahweh as the accused. Weiser (op. cit., p. 250) sees the
prophet to be calling the people to account, though "Er
kleidet dies in die Form des 'Rechtsstreits,' in dem Gott
zunächst in der Rolle des Angeklagten erscheint, als ob er
nicht gehalten habe, was er dem Volk versprochen hat." However, it is clear from vs. 2 that it is Yahweh who has the
complaint against Israel; i.e., Yahweh is plaintiff, Israel
the defendant (cp. Limburg, "ריב," p. 301). Vss. 3-5 are an
accusation and convey not so much the innocence of Yahweh
(though they do that, also), but the absolute and inexcusable
guilt of the defendant, Israel.

[2]Hillers, Covenant, p. 129; Westermann, Grundformen,
p. 144. Both compare Micah 6:3-5 to Jer. 2, where the charge
is explicit (see pp. 126-127, above).

consistent with what we find in 1:7, where Micah declares that
the symbols of Samaria's apostasy will be destroyed. The
"confession of culpability" in 6:7 ("my rebellion"; "my sin")
is of no help in securing the nature of the indictment, however, because it is devoid of content. Thus we would have:
the defendant is charged with and indicted for apostasy (6:3-
5) and acknowledges that he is guilty (of whatever he was
indicted for). Were we dealing in this passage with a "rib
absolu," we would be satisfied, for in two other examples of
this genre, Jer. 2 and Deut. 32, we find precisely: charged
with apostasy; indicted for apostasy; guilty of apostasy.[1]
We are, however, dealing with a "rib mitigé," another example
of which is Is. 1:2-4, 10-20.

According to Harvey, the difference between the "rib
mitigé" and the "rib absolu" is that, in the former, the
possibility for reconciliation between plaintiff and defendant
is left open--the conditions under which reconciliation is
possible being indicated by the Positive Decree: "Décret
positif indiqu(e) les conditions exigées pour la reprise de

---

[1]For Jer. 2, see pp. 126-127, above. In Deut. 32, the
charge implies apostasy (Interrogation, vs. 6); the defendant
is specifically indicted for apostasy (Historical Indictment,
vss. 7-15--especially vs. 15); the defendant is adjudged
guilty of apostasy (Declaration of Culpability, vs. 18).

relations."[1]

In our discussion of Is. 1, we did not consider the
Positive Decree. It appears in vss. 16-20, the first two
verses of which deserve our attention:[2]

Wash and be clean.
Take away from my sight the evil of your deeds.
Stop doing wrong. Learn to do right.
Seek justice. Straighten out the oppressor.
See that the orphan gets justice.
Take up the cause of the widow.[3]

We saw above (pp. 128-131) that that which Israel had done to
break the covenant was encapsulated in the phrase, "Your
hands are full of blood" (15c); here, that which will permit
reconciliation to take place, the covenant relationship to be

---

[1]Ibid., p. 53; cp., also, p. 55.

[2]Vss. 18-20 confirm the conditional nature of the
"rib." For the exegesis of these verses see Harvey, ibid.,
pp. 41-42. In essence he (following Fohrer) understands the
difficult vs. 18 as "une affirmation courante" in Israel,
while vss. 19-20 indicate ". . . à quelles conditions elle
est vraie" (p. 41). Thomas M. Raitt, "The Prophetic Summons
to Repentence," ZAW, 83 (1971), pp. 30-49, includes vss. 18-
20 in his list of examples of the "summons to repentenca"
form (p. 35). If Raitt is correct, and if vss. 18-20 are
part of the "rib," then the conditional nature of the "rib"
is confirmed not only by the "rib mitigé" form, but by its
concluding "summons to repentence" which urges the acceptance
of the conditions and warns against their rejection. We
would outline vss. 11-20 as follows: Israel has broken the
covenant (11-15); "Do this, and the covenant will be restored" (16-17); "Do it, will you?, or else!" (18-20).

[3]It is tempting to think of the imperatives of vss. 16-
17 as forming the protasis of a condition whose apodosis is
lacking (cp. G-K, 110f); i.e., "If you wash . . . (then, the
covenant relationship will be restored)."

restored,--that for which God pleads--is declared to be the removal of that blood, "Wash and be clean." And how is this cleansing to take place? By the doing of certain things ("Seek justice . . .") the antithesis of which apodictic law forbids (cp. pp. 130-131, above). From this we wish to make two points.

1. At least so far as the Isaiah passage is concerned, that which can prevent the dissolution of the covenant is behavior consonant with certain laws which appear in the Pentateuch in apodictic form. According to the Positive Decree, it is this designated behavior, and it alone, which can prevent the "rib mitige" from becoming a "rib absolu."

2. The content of the Positive Decree is related to the real basis of the charge of breach of covenant.[1] This is to be expected, since only when that which gave rise to the "rib" is ameliorated would it be reasonable for the "rib" to be dropped (i.e., bloodstained hands must be cleansed, wrongdoing be replaced by "rightdoing," the doing of injustice by justice).

It is this second point which relates to our discussion of Micah 6:1-8. We have been trying to ascertain from the

---

[1]Cp., also, the "rib mitige" of Is. 58:1-7. In vss. 2-4 it is declared to be the defendant's oppression and violence which have broken the covenant (note the root פשע in vs. 1!), while in the Positive Decree of vss. 5-7 it is the undoing of oppression and the relief of the oppressed which is enjoined. For the consonance of the real basis of the charge of breach of covenant with the Positive Decree of Micah 6:1-8, see below, pp. 139-143.

text what it is that Israel has done to cause God to insti-
ate the "r^ib." We have noted that others have deemed
apostasy to be the cause. If so·, we would expect this to be
reflected in the Positive Decree:

> And what does the Lord require of you
> Except your doing justice, loving faithfulness,
> And walking humbly with your God?

As Hillers has pointed out, the words משפט , חסד, and לכת
are at home in a covenant context--the latter two stressing
loyalty to the covenant and its Lord.[1] And, as far as the
latter words are concerned, it would be possible for the gist
of the "r^ib" to be: "You have committed apostasy (vss. 3-5),
. . . Now then, (give up your apostasy and) exhibit faithfulness to the covenant (אהבת חסד) and to God" (והצנע לכת
עם-אלהיך). What bothers us, however, is how to explain
עשות משפט with respect to apostasy as the cause of breach of
covenant. To express our quandary in the form of a question:
How would the doing of "justice" cause God to withdraw a

---

[1]Covenant, pp. 130-31. He says: "Hesed is the quality
one wants in a partner to an alliance, hence it involves
loyalty above all" (p. 130). And, with respect to לכת :
"Although it would be forced to call this word 'walk' technical legal language, since 'walk' is a common metaphor for
conduct of life, it is worth pointing out that 'walk,' especially in the phrase 'to walk after,' is used to describe the
relation of a vassal to his lord" (p. 131). For Hillers on
משפט, see p. 139, below. For the intimate connection of חסד
and covenant see, also, Norman H. Snaith, The Distinctive
Ideas of the Old Testament (New York: Schocken Books, 1964),
pp. 94-130, passim; e.g., "Unless this close and inalienable
connection with the idea of the covenant is realized, the
true meaning of chesed can never he understood" (p. 98).

"rib" which cites Israel for apostasy? We are inclined,
therefore, to look for something other than apostasy as the
cause of breach of covenant.

Yet, perhaps the very cause of our dilemma can aid in
its solution! If, in the "rib mitigé," that which the
Positive Decree urges represents the obverse of that which is
the real basis of the charge of breach of covenant (and
therefore " עשות משפט " makes us wary of its being apostasy
with which the defendant is charged and for which he is indicted in 6:3-5); then, if what will restore the covenant is
" עשות משפט ," it seems reasonable to infer that what has
broken the covenant is the defendant's failure vis-à-vis
משפט. But, what does it mean to "do משפט"? Norman Snaith's
study of the word leads him to conclude:

> It is necessary therefore to think of "doing mishpaṭ"
> (Micah 6:8) as meaning "doing God's will as it has
> been made clear in past experience."[1]

Where does one find that will? Delbert Hillers understands
Micah to assert its locus to be covenant law:

> God's first inescapable requirement is that the Is-
> raelites do "justice," Hebrew mishpat, a common term
> for the legal norms demanded by the covenant.[2]

To press still further: Where might one find these "legal
norms demanded by the covenant"? For Micah, the answer would

---

[1] Ibid., p. 76.

[2] Covenant, p. 130.

appear to be "apodictic law"; for, as we have already noted, Micah's accusations are grounded in apodictic law.[1] That is, whereas in his Prophetic Judgment-Speeches Micah singled out in his accusations acts which violated apodictic law and would bring disaster; here, in the "rîb mitige," he appeals to his hearers to fulfill the requirements of that law--using an epitome, "עשות משפט"--so that the "rîb" may be dropped and disaster forestalled.

From the Positive Decree of 6:8b-c, then, we infer that Israel has broken the covenant by failing to "do justice"; i.e., by acts contrary to apodictic law. But while this comports well with the rest of Micah's message, can 6:3-5, which contains the charge and indictment, bear the weight of this interpretation?

The most noticeable things about 6:3-5 are its contents and its tone. Its contents are a roll call of events of "Heilsgeschichte," the "צדקות יהוה." The tone suggests that these events ought to have evoked a certain response on the part of the recipient, and the gravamen of the charge and indictment is that the defendant did not so respond. Our look at 6:8b-c suggests that the expected response was that Israel would fulfill the requirements of apodictic law. We might, then, summarize the charge and indictment of 6:3-5 in

---

[1]See p. 65, above.

142

this way: "My gracious acts ought to have evoked obedience to the law, but they did not."

In his study of the root זכר, Brevard Childs considers the words, ". . . remember, . . . that you may acknowledge the righteous deeds of the Lord" (6:5), and approaches our view, in that he also sees Israel's failure as default in the realm of behavior:

> The act of remembering serves to actualize the past for a generation removed in time from those former events in order that they themselves can have an intimate encounter with the great acts of redemption. Remembrance equals participation. The present rupture in the relationship of Yahweh with his people stems from Israel's failure to understand the saving acts.
> . . . .
> . . . Precisely in these redemptive acts (sedhaqoth) he has revealed his righteousness (sedhaqah). But Israel has no understanding; she does not "know." In order to participate in this redemption, a righteous response is demanded.[1]

Further, assuming the correctness of our interpretation, this passage is not the only repository of the view that the proper response to "Heilsgeschichte" is obedience to the law. The Decalogue similarly predicates obedience to the

---

[1]Memory and Tradition, pp. 56-57. Cp., also, the comment of Johs. Pedersen in Israel: Its Life and Culture, I-II (London: Oxford University Press, 1959), pp. 106-07, which similarly connects remembering (זכר) and action: "When the soul remembers something, it does not mean that it has an objective memory image of some thing or event, but that this image is called forth in the soul and assists in determining its direction, its action. When man remembers God, he lets his being and his actions be determined by him. . . . To remember the works of Yahweh and to seek him, i.e. to let one's acts be determined by his will, is in reality the same.'

law as the requisite response to the divine beneficence: "I
am the Lord your God, who brought you forth from the land of
Egypt . . ." (cp. Micah 6:4) engenders, "You shall (not)
. . ." In the prophets, the locus classicus is Amos 2:6-11.
We have already had occasion to note that Israel's "rebellions" of 2:6-8 consist of the doing of things which apodictic law forbids (cp. pp. 106-109, above). In vss. 9 ff.,
Israel's rebellions are contrasted with the divine behavior
toward Israel: "But (the waw is adversative), as for me (the
pronoun is emphatic), I annihilated the Amorite before them
. . ."[1] In these verses, then, Amos says: "Time and again
Israel has disregarded the law; not a proper response for the
recipient of divine favor(s)."

We understand the charge and indictment of Micah 6:3-5
to be substantially the same as the indictment of Amos 2:6-11:
Israel has failed with respect to the demands of apodictic

---

[1]With respect to vss. 9-12, there is the question of
how much of these is to be attributed to Amos. Most of those
who deny the greater part of these verses to Amos refer to
Artur Weiser, Die Profetie des Amos (Giessen: Alfred
Töpelmann, 1929), pp. 93-96, where he argues that only vs. 9
(minus םהינפמ), which provides the connecting link between
vss. 6-8 and 13-16, originated with Amos. However, in his
later commentary on the Minor Prophets (op. cit., p. 122), it
is only vs. 12 which is designated a later addition. James
L. Mays (Amos, p. 45) accounts for the shift to direct address and the conventional style of vss. 10ff. on the grounds
that this is typical of "the recitation of Yahweh's classic
deeds." While we are inclined to ascribe at least vss. 9-11
to Amos, vs. 9, alone, following upon vss. 6-8 would still be
representative of the view that obedience to apodictic law is
the proper response to God's action in history on Israel's

law; a fact especially to be deplored when contrasted with the righteous deeds of Yahweh. The two passages differ, however, in that the indictment is explicit in Amos, while in Micah, the charge and indictment are implied by the tone and contents of the passage, and the implication confirmed by inference from the Positive Decree of 6:8b-c.

We have, then, in the "rîb mitigé" of 6:1-8: the defendant is charged with and indicted for (vss. 3-5) improper response to the יהוה צדקות (we infer that, as in Amos 2, the defendant has failed with respect to the demands of apodictic law); the defendant admits culpability (vs. 7); the possibility for reconciliation between defendant and plaintiff is left open, the condition necessary for the resumption of the relationship (which will be the consequence of the dropping of the lawsuit) being that the defendant rectify his behavior--i.e., that he "do justice" (vs. 8b-c). There is, then, the intelligible flow we have come to expect from our study of the "lawsuits" of Jeremiah 2 and Isaiah 1.

How are we to understand the Rejection of Sacrifices-- within which is found a "confession of culpability"--of vss. 6-8a? In the personal illustration which was recounted on p. 129 above, my doing dishes was an unsuccessful attempt to avert the punishment which I knew to be the consequence of my

behalf.

145

not spading the garden. It was my response to my recognition
that I was, in fact, guilty. The situation of vss. 6-8 is
similar. Culpability is recognized, and the issue is whether
and how the punishment can be averted. The answer is: "It
can. Not, however, by the device of offering sacrifices, but
only by ameliorating the wrong you have done." We understand
the prophet (speaking for the plaintiff, God) as the speaker
of vss. 6-7. He uses a "prophetic torah," placing in the
mouth of his audience the question--(You say), "With what
shall I come before the Lord, . . .?"--then, providing the
answer (vs. 8).[1]

We have now examined those prophetic passages which are
generally acknowledged to be "covenant lawsuits." We have
tried to ascertain in each instance what it was that the
accused had done which constituted breach of covenant; i.e.,
what the grounds for the lawsuit were. We saw that, in Jer.
2:4-13, Israel is declared guilty of apostasy--of behavior
which is prohibited by apodictic law--and that for this she
will be punished. In Is. 1:2-3, 10-20, the real guilt of

---

[1]Re the "prophetic torah," see Aage Bentzen, _Introduc-
tion to the Old Testament_, Vols. I-II (Copenhagen: Gad,
1959), I, pp. 201-02. With regard to the prophet as the
speaker of vss. 6-7, Harvey says: "On peut concevoir qu'il y
a véritable dialogue, comme en plusieurs autres cas vétéro-
testamentaires . . ., mais l'usage du _singulier_ rend beaucoup
plus probable la présence d'une tournure littéraire faisant
prononcer par le prophète lui-même cette phrase" (_op. cit._,
p. 44, fn. 2).

Israel is epitomized in the phrase of vs. 15c, "Your hands are full of blood." In these words are encapsulated all the crimes of which the prophet elsewhere declares Israel to be guilty. However, disaster can be averted, the lawsuit will be dropped, if Israel will but cleanse herself by doing certain things which apodictic law demands (see p. 136, above). The covenant need not be dissolved if Israel will exhibit faithfulness by observing the law. Micah 6:1-8 is similar to Isaiah 1. Here, Israel is declared not to have responded properly to God's saving acts. We have inferred that Israel's improper response has consisted of not "doing justice." If now she will but "do justice," the punishment will be averted and the covenant restored. Since elsewhere Micah's accusations are directed against those whose acts violate apodictic law, we understand his plea to be urging the reverse--that his hearers fulfill the requirements of that law.

Thus, both in its statement of those things which the defendant has done to break the covenant, and, in the "rîb mitigé," that which the defendant is urged to do to prevent the dissolution of the covenant, apodictic law seems to serve as the apparent standard in the "covenant lawsuit." This suggests to us once again that, for the prophets, the law was part of the covenant.

We have accumulated from our four prophets certain

features which are at home in a treaty context (treaty curse
parallels in Announcements of Disaster; the treaty conno-
tations of פשע and ידע; the "covenant lawsuit") and, joined
to these features, accusations or exhortations whose content
is paralleled in apodictic law.[1] We submit as the most probable explanation for this phenomenon that, for the prophets,
such law was part of a covenant conceived of as a treaty
between God and Israel. We do this partly because of mathematics, for we deem the occurrence of this phenomenon in four
different prophets to be significant. To the mathematics we
would add two other things which point to the same conclusion.

1. Such a view explains the divine concern for the behavior
of the people to which the prophets attest (they understand
themselves as sent to the people by God) and the ultimate
seriousness of that behavior.

When I am about to punish one of my children I will,
from time to time, use the following form: "I told you that
(you were to be in bed by 8:30) but you (stayed up until
9:00), therefore . . ." By placing the breaking of the commandment in the context of its promulgation I make my daughter aware not only that she has done something wrong, but
that the doing of it has disrupted our relationship. The

---

[1]Amos is missing the "covenant lawsuit" and Micah the
treaty connotation of ידע.

normal relationship between father and daughter, of which
fatherly beneficence is a characteristic, has now ceased to
exist. In this way, the real significance of the child's act
and its ultimate seriousness is made manifest (going to bed
half an hour late is no big deal--not obeying one's father
is).

In some such way we may understand the conjunction of
covenant elements and legal allusions in our prophets. The
prophets convey the divine concern for and the ultimate
seriousness of the people's disobedience by referring to the
context in which that disobedience is to be understood. It
is not just that the people have done something wrong, but
that their behavior has disrupted a relationship. The normal
relationship between God and Israel, of which divine beneficence and protection is a characteristic, has now ceased to
exist (not seeing that the poor get justice may be no big
deal--not obeying a covenant stipulation is; or, to turn it
around, seeing that the poor get justice _is_ a big deal _be-_
cause it is a covenant stipulation).
2. That the requirements of apodictic law are to be understood as covenant stipulations also explains what we noted in
the first part of this chapter; _that_ _it_ _is_ _God_ _who_ _acts_ _to_
enforce _the_ _law._ Just as the king of Israel musters his
troops when his vassal rebels:

> . . . when the king of Moab rebelled (ויפשע) against
> the king of Israel. King Jehoram immediately marched

out from Samaria and mustered all Israel.
(II Kings 3:5b-6)

so God musters his troops when his vassal, Israel, disobeys

the law:

> But as for me, I am filled with power,
> With the spirit of the Lord,
> And with justice and might,
> To declare to Jacob his rebellion (פשעו),
> To Israel his sin (Micah 3:8).

Having considered the nature and authority of "The

Law in the Prophets," we must now go on to see who is bound

by the law.

III.   THE PEOPLE OF THE LAW IN THE PROPHETS

In our first chapter we argued that prophetic accusation assumed a standard by which the accused was judged and
to which he was bound, and that where a law (or laws) could
be seen to have comprised that standard, the Pentateuchal
form of that law was always apodictic. In the second chapter
we went on to inquire into the grounds on which the prophets
understood this law to be binding. Our answer was that it
was seen as part of a covenant which was conceived of as a
treaty between God and Israel. To transgress the law was to
break the covenant, from which would ensue the punitive
action of the covenant suzerain, Yahweh, against the transgressor.

In this chapter we turn to our final question regarding
the law as it is to be inferred from our four prophets--the
identity of those of whom obedience to the law is expected.
Once again we are faced with the necessity of using an in-
direct method to arrive at an answer. Our situation is analogous to that of a man who, wishing to learn whether he must
pay income tax, is hindered by an inability to obtain a copy
of the requisite laws. Suddenly an alternative way of
gaining the information occurs to him. He will find out who

151

has been indicted for income tax evasion and learn all that
he can about them. The procedure is a bit tedious because of
all the court cases he must wade through, and it is not fool-
proof because in some instances the liability of the accused
may be at issue; yet, lacking a copy of the laws, it is the
best available way. Similarly, by scrutinizing those passages in our prophets where the indictment seems to be
grounded in apodictic law for the identity of the accused and
any features which may help to characterize him, we may be
able to infer who, according to the prophets, is bound by the
law. We will look at each of our prophets in turn.

The people of the law in Amos

The following are the relevant passages: 2:6-8; 3:9-11; 4:1-
3; 5:7, 10-12; 6:12; 8:4-6.[1]

In 2:6-8, the accused is "Israel" (2:6). We are immediately inclined to identify this "Israel" as the northern
kingdom for three reasons.

1. According to 7:13, Amos has appeared at Bethel and prophesied there. The issue, according to 7:10-17 is whether the
northern kingdom may continue as his prophetic domain.[2] The

---

[1]For apodictic law as the "Begründung" for the accusations recorded in these passages, see above, pp. 97-100,
106-109, and Bach, "Gottesrecht," passim.

[2]Cp. James M. Ward, Amos & Isaiah: Prophets of the
Word of God (Nashville and New York: Abingdon Press, 1969),
p. 30, fn. 14: ". . . the issue according to 7:10-17 was

natural assumption is that the audience and the accused are one, i.e., the northern kingdom.

2. Since the other accused of 1:3-2:16 are political entities, the same must be true of the "Israel" of 2:6. The mention of Judah in 2:4, if original, further confirms this.[1] If the Judah oracle is a later addition, its inclusion signifies that the redactor understood the "Israel" of 2:6 as the northern kingdom.

3. In other places in Amos, "Israel" is clearly a political designation (e.g., 7:9-10). To this may be added that in several unambiguous passages it is the northern kingdom or places within its boundaries which are to suffer the destructive effects of Yahweh's wrath (e.g., 3:9-11; 3:12; 5:5b; 6:13-14; 7:9). The assumption of prophetic proclamation is that divine judgment is not desultory but the consequence of sufficient cause; therefore, the object of destruction must also be the subject of provocation--i.e., the northern kingdom.

May we, then, declare the "Israel" of 2:6 to be the northern kingdom? Not without further reflection, for in

---

whether Amos was to prophesy in the kingdom of Israel. The command attributed to God in vs. 15 was therefore clearly meant to obligate Amos to do so. In vss. 10, 11, 16, and 17, 'Israel' obviously means the northern kingdom."

[1] Probably, however, the Judah strophe is not original. See, e.g., Eissfeldt, *Introduction*, p. 400, and many others.

several passages "Israel" is qualified by reference to a heritage which is not the exclusive property of the northern
kingdom, but is shared with her southern neighbor. This
"Israel" is declared to have been brought up by Yahweh from
"the land of Egypt" (3:1; 9:7), to have been in the wilderness
forty years (5:25), and to be related by covenant to Yahweh
(3:2). This "Israel" is defined not politically and geo-
graphically, but historically and religiously. Or, if one
must find a political and geographical equivalent for this
"Israel," it is the kingdoms of Israel and Judah.

Our problem is the identity of the "Israel" of 2:6 who
is the "accused" of 2:6-8. In 2:9-11 this "Israel" is defined in historical terms akin to those of the "Israel" discussed in the preceding paragraph. Thus, it is the conviction of Moses Buttenwieser that:

> Since . . . the whole nation shared in these acts of
> God's favor (2:9-10), it is obvious that throughout
> the passus II, 6-16 the prophet had the whole nation
> in mind, i.e., Judah as well as Israel.[1]

We are willing to go along with Buttenwieser, but only
part of the way. To indicate the extent of our agreement and
the point at which we demur, let us imagine ourselves among

---

[1]The Prophets of Israel (New York: The MacMillan Company, 1914), pp. 232-33. It is Buttenwieser's view that,
except where Amos ". . . directs his utterances against his
North-Israelitish hearers specifically" (p. 234), his proph-
ecies are addressed to "Israel and Judah alike." He argues
his case on pp. 225-39. Our disagreement is advanced on the
following pages.

154

Amos' auditors at Bethel. As he denounces our enemies, he
wins our assent and admiration. Then, the trap is sprung:
"For the three rebellions of Israel . . ." Unlike the twen-
tieth century scholar, we need not pause to inquire as to the
denotation of the word "Israel"; set beside Damascus, Gaza,
etc., it can only mean the northern kingdom. But, and here
Buttenwieser is correct, the historical retrospect of vss. 9-
10 does something to the "Israel" of vs. 6. However, the
references to Conquest, Wilderness, and Exodus do not (as
Buttenwieser would have it) redefine the "accused" to include
Judah (i.e., give "Israel" a different denotation), but indicate the grounds on which the behavior of the "accused"
(recounted in 2:6-8) may be deemed "accusable" (i.e.,
"Israel" is given a connotation).

There are, in Amos, two "Israels": 1) a nation--the
northern kingdom--called Israel; 2) that which we will designate 'Israel,' a people with a history (Exodus, Wilderness,
Conquest)--a people related by covenant to Yahweh.[1] In Amos'
day, there are two repositories of 'Israel'; Israel and
Judah. Amos accuses Israel, in God's name, and announces her

---

[1]This is not to deny the northern kingdom a history,
but the history which Amos recalls is not the unique possession of the northern kingdom. For a discussion of the
terms עם and גוי, see E. A. Speiser, "'People' and 'Nation'
of Israel," _JBL_, LXXIX (1960), pp. 157-63. John Bright argues
that, as the subject of a history, the proper classification
for 'Israel' is as a people (_Early Israel_, pp. 113-14).

coming judgment. Amos defends this divine prerogative on the
ground that Israel embodies 'Israel.' The "Israel" of 2:6 is
Israel; but, as 2:9-10 shows, she is accused because she is
also 'Israel.'

We can arrive at the view that the "Israel" who is
"accused" in 2:6 is to be understood as the northern kingdom
(and not Judah as well as Israel) in another way. As Amos'
auditors (the majority of whom were citizens of the northern
kingdom) heard his message unfold (we are thinking, now, of
the totality of oracles which may be attributed to Amos),
they would have been struck by two things: 1) it is, pre-
dominantly, northern sites and the northern kingdom whose
destruction is specified (e.g., 3:9-11; 3:12; 5:5b; 6:13-14;
7:9);[1] 2) it is they (the auditors) to whom the indictments
are addressed (cp. the ringing "you" of 5:7, 11-12; 6:12; 8:4-
6). Now, if you were among Amos' auditors--enraged by the
announcements of the coming destruction of your capital and
cult places, and angered by the prophet's accusing "you";
would you want to know, "who else" (is going to be destroyed/
is accused), or "why" (we are going to be destroyed/are being

---

[1]We are aware of the reference to "those who are at
ease in Zion" (6:1), but are content with the explanation of
Mays (Amos, p. 115): "The inclusion of Zion in the opening
line is surprising for a prophet who elsewhere appears to
speak only to the northern kingdom. But the shoe fits people
in Jerusalem as well as in Samaria; in the general impersonal
style of the woe-saying Amos has simply begun in an inclusive
fashion."

accused)? We submit that the latter is your query, and that
it is the question "why?" that the historical retrospect of
2:9-10 and the "Israel" juxtaposed with allusions to Exodus
(3:1; 9:7), Wilderness (5:25), and covenant (3:2) answer.
These represent Yahweh's credentials, his claim upon the northern kingdom, his right to come in judgment.

Our understanding of the identity of the "you" who are
accused in 5:7, 11-12; 6:12; and 8:4-6 has been touched upon
in the preceding paragraph. They are Amos' auditors; residents of Israel. (However, we would not limit the "you" to
the members of Amos' audience. His words are intended for all
the citizens of Israel. Similarly, when President Nixon says,
"my fellow Americans," he addresses his words not only to his
"live" audience, but to all who may be so addressed.) Thus,
as in 2:6-8, so in these verses, the citizens of the northern
kingdom are the "accused"; but, again, in the context of Amos'
total message, they are "accused" because they are citizens
of 'Israel.'

So, too, with the accusations against the inhabitants
of Samaria (3:9-11) and the Samaritan women (4:1-3). It is
because they are 'Israelites' that they may be singled out for
judgment (cp. 3:1-2).

Who, then, according to Amos, are the people of the law?
Those whom he accuses of transgressing the law are the inhabitants of Israel (2:6-8; 5:7, 10-12; 6:12; 8:4-6) and groups

within Israel (3:9-11; 4:1-3). However, as we have seen, the presupposition of their accusation is that they are 'Israel' --have received the benefits of Yahweh's saving deeds and are related by covenant to him. Thus, for Amos, the people of the law (to set the grammar straight) is 'Israel.'

The people of the law in Micah

Those passages in which accusations grounded in apodictic law appear are: 2:1-5; 2:8-10; 3:1-4; 3:9-12; 5:9-13; 6:1-8; 6:9-16; 7:1-6.[1] We accept the conclusions of Eissfeldt, who attributes them all to Micah.[2]

With regard to the oracles in question, our present concern is to learn the identity of the accused, in the hope that, from what is said of them, we may ascertain whom Micah understands to be bound by the law. With respect to this concern, the oracles in chapters two and three may immediately be separated from the remaining passages, for, in these, it is various groups (who may, with greater or lesser precision, be

---

[1]For the correspondence of the content of these accusations to laws in apodictic form, see Beyerlin, Kult-traditionen, pp. 54-64, and the table on pp. 179-180, below. We have inferred that it is Israel's failure to observe apodictic law for which she is indicted in 6:1-8 (cp. p. 140, above). We have chosen to omit the implied accusation of idolatry in 1:7 for reasons already stated (see pp. 110-111, above).

[2]Introduction, pp. 409-12.

identified) whom the prophet denounces.[1] Those who are indicted appear to be inhabitants of Jerusalem, since it is
said that the consequence of their acts is to be the destruc·
tion of Jerusalem (3:12), a city which is being built on the
insecure foundation of bloodshed and violence (3:10).[2] And,
since they are citizens of the southern kingdom, how strange
that Micah should address them so:

> Hear this, you heads of the house of Jacob
> And rulers of the house of Israel . . .
> (3:9; cp. 3:1; 2:7)

Can it be that, for Micah, Jacob/Israel can designate

---

[1]E.g., the wealthy landlords in 2:1-4 (and probably 2:
8-10), and priests and prophets in 3:11. The identification
of the קצינים/ראשים of 3:1 and 3:9 is more difficult. Are
these two groups or one? We assume that it is the leadership
in general which is addressed by these terms; in part because
they appear to be delineated in 3:11 as judges, priests, and
prophets, and in part because קצין in Isaiah 3:6-7 appears to
mean simply "leader" (for a society which is bereft of leadership; cp. 3:2-4). For a different view which sees these as
termini technici, see Beyerlin, Kulttraditionen, pp. 52-53.
For our purposes, the identity of these groups doesn't matter; only that they were recognizable entities to Micah's
auditors, and that (as we shall see on p. 160, below) those
who comprise these groups are members of the covenant community.

[2]Fohrer (Introduction, p. 444), for example, sees the
sayings of these chapters as "directed against the ruling
classes and cult prophets in Jerusalem" (underlining ours).
The phrasing of the latter part of our sentence (". . . a
city which is being built . . .") is a "steal" from Rolland
E. Wolfe's exegesis of 3:10 in The Book of Micah, IB, Vol. VI,
p. 920: ". . . civil violence, corruption, and crime . . .
had become the basis on which Jerusalem, and the nation of
which it was the nucleus, was being built. Micah warned that
this made a very insecure foundation for the future of any
city or nation."

Judah? Apparently, but not exclusively:[1]

> All this, for Jacob's rebellion,
> For the house of Israel's sins.
> What is Jacob's rebellion?
> Is it not Samaria (1:5a-b)?

Here, the mention of Samaria indicates that Jacob/Israel may

---

[1]In passages which are attributed by Eissfeldt to
Micah, Jacob/Israel occur in parallelism four times (1:5; 3:
1, 8, 9), while Jacob occurs alone twice (1:5; 2:7) and
Israel four times (1:13, 14, 15; 6:2). The way these are
used by Micah seems to us very much like the way the English
use the word "America(n)." When we were in England some
years ago, and I was asked where I was from, I would usually
answer, "I'm an American"; whereupon I would be asked, "From
the United States or Canada?" For them, "America" was a
continental designation (actually it designates two contin-
ents; but, since I spoke English, South American was elim-
inated); therefore, to learn my national identity, another
question was necessary. Still (let it be noted), my answer
was not incorrect; for (as even my English questioner would
have had to admit), a citizen of the United States is, indu-
bitably, an American. The situation is similar with respect
to our terms in Micah: as we shall see, their primary significance is covenantal (rather than continental), not national. If we wish to learn whether it is the northern kingdom or the southern kingdom that is being spoken of or addressed (as Jacob/Israel, or as Jacob or Israel), we must
look at the context (cp. my English questioner's being com-
pelled to ask a second question to learn my national identity). And, with the exception of 1:5, 1:13, and 6:2, context indicates that the one spoken of or addressed as Jacob/
Israel (or as Jacob or Israel) is clearly Judah/Jerusalem.
We think that, in 6:1-8 also, Judah/Jerusalem is being addressed, for the second person predominates (cp. vss. 3-5,
8), and it is natural to think of the equation: Israel (6:2)
equals "you" (6:3) equals the prophet's auditors (i.e., the
inhabitants of Jerusalem). Just as clearly, however, the
mention of Samaria in 1:5 (see the following footnote) and
the Announcement of Judgment (1:6) indicate that, in 1:5, the
northern kingdom is being spoken of. We do not understand
the "Israel" of 1:13; indeed, we do not understand 1:13.

be used of the northern kingdom.[1] Now, if the terms Jacob/
Israel can be referred by Micah in one place to one nation and
in another to another, we submit that an intolerable burden
is placed upon a listener who would ascertain a national signification from Micah's use of these terms. But, perhaps
that is the point: for Micah, the primary significance of
these terms is not national.

Earlier in our study we dealt at length with the idea
that, for our four prophets, פשע was a treaty expression which
signified that a treaty had been violated (pp. 104-116).
From this it follows that, in our prophets, the subject of
פשע when it is a verb, or its nomen rectum when it is a noun
in the construct state will identify the defaulting covenant
partner. Let us refresh our memory as to Micah 1:5a; now,
however, nothing less than the Hebrew text will do:

בפשע יעקב כל-זאת ובחטאות בית ישראל

Notice! פשע is a nomen regens. יעקב is its nomen rectum.
And, ישראל (בית) is in parallelism with יעקב. In this passage, then, Jacob/Israel is the name of the people which has
broken the covenant; that is, these terms serve Micah as

---

[1]Following Beyerlin, Kulttraditionen, pp. 13-14, and
Artur Weiser, The Old Testament: Its Formation and Development (New York: Association Press, 1961), p. 253, and understanding the reference to Judah and Jerusalem in 1:5 as an
addition. Thus 1:5, which has both Jacob/Israel in parallelism and Jacob alone, concerns only the northern kingdom.

161

appellatives for the covenant people.

Thus, to return to chapter three of Micah, the leaders who are accused, though they are residents of Jerusalem, are addressed as leaders of "the house of Jacob/Israel," for it is by this address that Micah reminds them that it is their membership in the covenant people that places them under obligation to the law. In the second and third chapters, then, the accused are various groups whose residence is Jerusalem. From the third chapter we learn that what makes such groups liable for judgment is their citizenship in (i.e., the individuals of which the group is comprised are citizens of) the covenant community.

So far in Micah, the people of the law is the covenant people, bearers of the name Jacob/Israel. Is this the same people whom, in our study of Amos, we called 'Israel'? Apparently so, for in the covenant lawsuit of 6:1-8, the defendant, Israel (6:2), is said to have been the recipient of צדקות יהוה (6:3-5), among which was the "bringing forth from Egypt" (6:4), of which Amos' 'Israel' (or rather, Israel, being a repository of 'Israel') was also the beneficiary (Amos 2:10; 3:1; 9:7).

There is nothing in the remaining oracles (5:9-13; 6:9-16; 7:1-6) to gainsay the results of our study of chapters two and three that, for Micah, the people of the law is the covenant community. There are, however, other differences.

162

These oracles convey the impression of a "lawlessness" run
rampant; extending to the religious life of the people (5:12-
13 imply that they are guilty of idolatry), and even into the
home (7:6; cp. esp. Deut. 27:16). Further, whereas in the
earlier chapters it was the leaders who were addressed, in
these, it seems as if the moral turpitude of the elite has
infected the entire community, so that "the city" has now become the addressee (6:9). Indeed, it is precisely Micah's
estimate that all are guilty:

> The faithful man[1] has vanished from the land,
> None upright among men (7:2a).

Micah begins by denouncing the leaders; then, the
entire community becomes the object of his imprecations.
Still, it is qua covenant community that they are culpable,
for it is to the covenant people that Micah's prophetic au-
thorization extends:

> But as for me, I am filled with power . . .
> To declare to Jacob his rebellion,
> To Israel his sin (3:8).

---

[1]"The faithful man" represents our translation of the
Hebrew חסיד. The one who is חסיד is faithful to the covenant
(cp. Jer. 3:12); i.e., exhibits חסד (cp. Snaith, Distinctive
Ideas, p. 123). We saw that, according to 6:8, one of the
things which God requires as a condition for withdrawing his
lawsuit against Israel is her אהבת חסד (exhibiting faithfulness to the covenant and its Lord; see p. 138, above). In 7:
1-6, Micah uses a variety of images to convey the desperate
situation of his people. So bleak is it that, while God
requires אהבת חסד of them if they wish to avert disaster,
according to 7:2, the land is bereft of even one person to
fulfill the divine stipulation.

The people of the law in Isaiah

With respect to the Isaianic material our procedure
must differ from that adopted for Amos and Micah, for here we
have no Bach or Beyerlin on whom to rely for establishing the
correspondence in content of the prophet's accusations to laws
in apodictic form (the necessary preliminary to ascertaining
the identity of the accused). Therefore, we must assume the
obligation of examining Isaiah's Prophetic Judgment-Speeches
and variants thereof for accusations grounded in apodictic
law. For convenience, we may begin with those of Isaiah's
accusations which decry social injustice in general and/or in
specific instances thereof.

Isaiah uses an astonishing variety of forms to convey
his charges of injustice, all of which appear in the first
ten chapters: Covenant Lawsuit (1:2-3, 10-20); Lament (1:21-
23); Lawsuit (3:13-15); Parable (5:1-7); Woe-Speech (5:8-10,
22-24; 10:1-4). That which is indicted includes: oppression
(1:17; 3:15; 10:1); not defending the orphan and widow (1:17;
1:23; 10:2); murder (1:21); accepting bribes (1:23; 5:23);
robbery (3:14); a covetousness (?) that issues in an unwar-
ranted accumulation of property (5:8-10; cp. Mic. 2:1-4); perversion of justice (5:23; 10:2).[1] Apodictic prohibitions

---

[1]For a detailed treatment of the accusations of 1:2-4,
10-20; 1:21-23; and 3:13-15 and their basis in apodictic law,
see above, pp. 127-131, p. 87 (fn. 1), and pp. 85-86, respectively.

which correspond in content to these indictments are: oppression (Lev. 19:13a); oppression of orphan and widow (Ex. 22:20-21; Deut. 24:17; 27:19); murder (Ex. 20:13); bribery (Deut. 16:19); robbery (Lev. 19:13a); covetousness (Ex. 20: 17) and invasion of property rights (Deut. 27:17); perversion of justice (Ex. 23:1-4; Deut. 16:19).

In these accusations of social injustice, both the community in general and/or specific groups are accused. Examples of the former are "Israel" (1:3), "a once faithful city" (1:21), and the "house of Israel"/"men of Judah" (5:7). Various leaders are among those groups frequently indicted: e.g., "rulers" (1:10), "princes" (1:23; 3:14), and "elders" (3:14). Other groups are delineated not by a titular designation, but by what they have done (e.g., "those who acquit the guilty for a bribe"; 5:23. Cp. 5:8; 10:1). The Woe-Speech serves as the formal vehicle for this type of "anonymous" group-indictment.[1]

In addition to these acts of social injustice, Isaiah's denunciations of idolatry and the alliance with Egypt are also grounded in apodictic law.

Idolatry comes under indictment in 2:6-21 (cp. 2:8, 18,

---

[1]Cp. Westermann, Grundformen, p. 138: ". . . beziehen sich die Wehe-Worte nie auf das ganze Volk; selten auf bestehende Gliederungen des Volkes, also Priester, Propheten o. ä.; das Wehe gilt denen, die jetzt gerade etwas Bestimmtes tun." See, also, Erhard Gerstenberger, "The Woe-Oracles of the Prophets," JBL, LXXXI (1962), pp. 251-52.

20).[1] The apodictically formulated laws of Lev. 26:1 and 19:
4 prohibit the making and worship of idols. The "accused" in
this passage is "thy people, the house of Jacob" (2:6).

Isaiah denounces the negotiations for an alliance with
Egypt during the reign of Hezekiah in three oracles: 28:14-
15, 17b-22; 30:1-5; 31:1-3.[2] While foreign alliances are not
explicitly prohibited in apodictic law, the prohibition of
other deities (Ex. 20:3) may have had as its understood corollary the rejection of foreign alliances.[3] Whatever the

---

[1]Yehezkel Kaufmann in The Religion of Israel, tr. and
abridged by Moshe Greenberg (Chicago: The University of Chicago Press, 1960), p. 382, considers the following "proph-
ecies concerning idolatry" to emanate from the prophet: 2:8,
18, 20; 17:8; 27:9; 30:22; 31:7. Once again, we follow
Eissfeldt, who considers only the verses from chapter 2 to be
Isaiah's (Introduction, pp. 308-17). Some commentators (e.g.,
Gray, Isaiah, p. 302) find, in 17:10, an allusion to the
Adonis cult, seeing in the verse an indictment of idolatry/
apostasy. This is by no means certain. For an alternative
view of 17:10-11, cp. Kissane, Isaiah, I, pp. 192-93. In an
oracle against Assyria (10:5-11), God announces that he will
deal with "Jerusalem and her idols" as he has dealt with
"Samaria and her images" (10:11).
     Returning to chapter two, 2:6 presents textual problems
(see commentaries). If one reads with BH[3] וֹעֹנְנִים וקֹסְמִים, then
we have an additional accusation grounded in apodictic law.
Both are prohibited by Deut. 18:10, and the latter by Lev. 19:
26. The major thrust of our passage, however, is the indictment of idolatry and pride. Pride is denounced in several
places by Isaiah (cp. 3:16-24; 5:21; 9:9; 28:1-4), and is
characteristic of his message.

[2]For the delimitation of these oracles, see Brevard S.
Childs, Isaiah and the Assyrian Crisis (London: SCM Press,
1967), pp. 28-31, 32-35. He argues, on form-critical grounds,
that 28:16-17a is a "secondary redactional element" (pp. 30-
31).

[3]So Mendenhall, Law and Covenant, p. 38: ". . . the
first obligation of the covenant was to reject all foreign

166

commandment, itself, may have implied, it is probable that

Isaiah understood the alliance with Egypt as an act of

apostasy:

> Woe to those who go down to Egypt for aid,
> Relying on horses,
> They trust in chariots because they are many
> In horsemen because they are very strong,
> But they have no regard for the Holy One of Israel
> The Lord they do not consult (31:1).

Isaiah declares the choice of Egypt to be a rejection of God.

But, how abortive is the apostasy:

> The Egyptians are men, not God (31:3)!

Bruce Vawter also understands Isaiah's indictment of foreign

alliances to be, at bottom, an indictment for apostasy:

> Foreign alliances were wrong not because foreigners
> were necessarily a scurvy lot. Rather, such alliances
> implied repudiation of Israel's alliance with Yahweh
> . . . They were wrong because they subverted the theo-
> cratic society of which Yahweh was head and author,
> substituting an alien partner from whom protection was
> sought and to whom loyalty and fealty were due instead
> of to Yahweh's law.[1]

Thus, while Isaiah's denunciations of the alliance with Egypt

do not exhibit the verbal correspondences to apodictic law

that are present in his accusations of social injustice and

---

relations--i.e. with other gods, and by implication, with
other political groups." Mendenhall explains that for Israel
to "make covenants with their neighbors . . . would be to
recognize the pagan deities as witnesses and guarantors of
the covenant" (p. 38). Cp. also Phillips, Criminal Law, p.
39.

[1]The Conscience of Israel (New York: Sheed & Ward,
1961), pp. 190-91.

idolatry, they are rooted in that commandment wherein Yahweh demands that he, alone, be suzerain of his people. Those to whom this apostate behavior is imputed are the rulers (28:14).

We have now completed our examination of those Prophetic Judgment-Speeches of Isaiah whose accusations are grounded in apodictic law in search of the identity of the "accused." As with Amos and Micah, the defendant varies: sometimes Isaiah accuses the entire community; at other times, it is groups ("anonymous" or specified) who are placed under indictment.

When we ask what it is about the accused that makes them subject to the law, a phenomenon which we observed in Micah affords a clue: Isaiah, too, can refer to the people of Judah and Jerusalem as "Israel."[1] The identity is established by parallelism in the final verse of the parable of 5:1-7:

The vineyard of the Lord of hosts

---

[1] For Micah's use of (Jacob)/Israel with reference to Judah and the conclusions which we drew from it, see above, pp. 157-160. For the discussion to follow and for additional instances of Isaiah's use of "Israel" to refer to Judah, see Walther Eichrodt, "Prophet and Covenant: Observations on the Exegesis of Isaiah," in Proclamation and Presence, ed. by John I. Durham and J. R. Porter (Richmond: John Knox Press, 1970), pp. 170-72. That Isaiah does think of Judah (and the northern kingdom as well) as 'Israel' is confirmed by 8:14, where he speaks of "both houses of Israel." Eichrodt defends the MT of 8:14 as follows: "The fact that the expression is unique suggests that we should not prefer the easier reading of the LXX: 'the house of Jacob'" (p. 172).

Is the house of Israel,
The men of Judah
His cherished plant (5:7).

However, for Isaiah, not only the people of Judah but their God can bear the attribute "of Israel." In a recent study, Walther Eichrodt points out that "the designation of God as 'the Holy One of Israel' . . . is characteristic of Isaiah," and also calls attention to the title, "the Mighty One of Israel" (1:24).[1]

Eichrodt emphasizes that Isaiah's linking of the name "Israel" with Judah antedated the fall of Samaria, and that this use was available to the prophet because the name had a significance in addition to its political signification:

> It was not because the name "Israel" had become available after the fall of Samaria that the prophet could venture to claim it for Judah, but because this name also had, as well as its political significance as a designation for the Northern Kingdom, a religious and theocratic significance, going back before the creation of the state, as the description of the people of Yahweh to whom Judah also belonged.[2]

Isaiah's use of the name "Israel" to signify the covenant people or to identify its God is found three times in the context of passages in which the defendant's indictment is grounded in apodictic law.

In 1:21-23, Jerusalem, the "once faithful city," and its princes are indicted for various acts prohibited by

---

[1] Ibid., pp. 169-70.

[2] Ibid., p. 171.

apodictic law (see pp. 87 and 162-163, above); for which,
they will experience judgment. The agent of that judgment is
to be "the Lord of hosts, the Mighty One of Israel" (1:24).
"The Lord of hosts" was the name of God current in Judah:
by identifying this God further as "the Mighty One of Israel,"
Isaiah is able to convey that it is as God of the covenant
people that the divine executioner comes.[1] Since it is the
God of the people of the covenant who executes judgment upon
those who have transgressed the law, we infer that, for
Isaiah, it is the covenant people who are bound by the law.

We have shown above that it is probable that Isaiah
saw the alliance with Egypt as an act of apostasy (p. 165),
a choosing of Egypt rather than God. Notice, then, the name
of the God whom Isaiah declares the anonymous defendants to
have rejected: ". . . they have no regard for the Holy One
of Israel" (31:1). From the knowledge that it is the God of
the covenant people from whom the defendants are accused of
being apostate, it is but a short step to the inference that
it is because they are members of the covenant community that
the defendants are "accusable."

---

[1]This observation proceeds from Eichrodt's comment on
the presence of יהוה צבאות (". . . the great name of God
current in Judah . . .") in 17:3, followed by אלהי ישראל
in 17:6; the intent of Isaiah's use of the latter being to
". . . characterize the coming annihilation expressly as the
work of the God who does not spare, on the grounds of favour-
itism, the people chosen and sanctified by him . . ." (p.
171).

Finally, in the Covenant Lawsuit of 1:2-3, 10-20, while it is the rulers and people of Jerusalem who are under indictment (1:10), in the prosecution's opening statement where the case is summarized succinctly it is said that:

Israel does not know,
My people does not understand (1:3b).

That is, it is their identity as 'Israel' that subjects the defendants to trial; it is the fact that they embody the covenant community that binds them to the law.[1]

Like Amos and Micah, Isaiah confronts the people as a whole and groups among them with specific examples of their failure vis-à-vis the law. Not in every instance does Isaiah indicate what it is about those whom he accuses that makes them responsible to the law; yet, he does remind them that they are 'Israel,' that it is "the Holy One of Israel" whom they have forsaken (cp. 1:4), and that it is "the Mighty One of Israel" who effects judgment against them. From this we conclude that for Isaiah, too, the people of the law is 'Israel.' In Isaiah, 'Israel's' defection from its covenant relationship with Yahweh is characterized in terms of the son's rebellion against his father (1:2-3; 30:1) rather than

---

[1]We have treated the question of the relationship of the accusation in this Covenant Lawsuit to apodictic law on pp. 127-131, above.

as an improper response to "Heilsgeschichte."[1]

The people of the law in Jeremiah

As for our eighth century prophets, for Jeremiah too,
the people of the law is the covenant people, 'Israel.' 2:4-
4:2 (omitting 3:6-18) and the "temple sermon" (7:1-15)
exhibit features akin to, and which we found to be significant in, the message of his prophetic predecessors.[2]

2:4-4:2 contains a series of utterances, directed to
the people of Judah, whose subject matter is apostasy.[3]
But, though it is Judah's apostasy which is denounced, and
her repentence urged (3:22; 4:1), she is referred to and addressed as "Israel": "house of Jacob, and all the families
of the house of Israel" (2:4); "Israel" (2:14, 31; 3:23;

---

[1]See above, p. 117, for the use of the father-son
analogy to express the covenant relationship.

[2]While in dealing with the subject of apostasy 3:6-18
is at one with the rest of 2:4-4:2, in nomenclature it is
not, for the "Israel" in it is clearly the exiled northern
kingdom. Beginning with 3:19 ff., "Israel," as elsewhere in
the section, signifies Judah. Cp. Rudolph, Jeremia, p. 25:
"3:19 ff. schliesst weder an 3:14-18 noch . . . an 3:12 f.
an, weil nach der Begnadigung von Israel und Juda nicht noch
einmal der Vorwurf der Untreue (20) erhoben werden kann,
sondern ist Fortsetzung von 3:1-5 . . . ('Haus Israel' in 20,
'Söhne Israels' in 21, 'Israel' in 23 und 4:1 meint Juda wie
in 2:26, (3), 14, 31)."

[3]It is interesting in light of our discussion of
Isaiah's attitude to foreign alliances (pp. 164-166, above),
that Jeremiah clearly labels them apostasies (cp. 2:17-19).

172

4:1); "house of Israel" (2:26; 3:20); "Israel's sons" (3:21).[1]
It would seem that, for Jeremiah, Judah's apostasy and her
being "Israel" had something to do with one another; that her
identity was connected with her culpability.

In the Covenant Lawsuit of 2:4-13, the defendant's
apostasy is set in a particular context:

> What disability did your fathers find in me
> That they abandoned me
> . . .
> They did not say, "Where is the Lord
> Who brought us up from the land of Egypt,
> Who led us in the wilderness
> . . ."
> Though I brought you to a garden land
> To enjoy its bounteous produce,
> You entered and defiled my land,
> Turning my heritage into an abomination.
> (2:5-7)

Like father, like son: both have committed apostasy, and the
apostasy of each is contrasted with deeds of Yahweh of which
each has been a beneficiary. There is continuity: one Lord;
one people; one story. The people is "Israel" (2:4), and
"Israel" is bound to be faithful. But, she was not, and is
not.

The "temple sermon" is delivered as a message from "the
Lord of hosts, the God of Israel" (for the significance of
the title in Isaiah, see p. 168, above) to "all Judah" (7:2-
3). As the consequence of "the wickedness of (his) people
Israel" was, at one time, that God destroyed Shiloh (7:12);

---

[1]"O Judah" (2:28) is the solitary exception.

173

so now, as a consequence of "all Judah's" having done things
which are prohibited by the "ten commandments" (7:9), the
same God will destroy the temple (7:14). As for the people,
themselves; their fate is to be the same as that of their
"kinsmen, all the progeny of Ephraim" (7:15). In this passage, then, the people who are declared to have transgressed
the law (and therefore, by implication, must be bound by it)
are: 1) addressed by, and to be punished by, "the God of
Israel"; 2) linked in transgression and by fate to "my people
Israel"; 3) "kinsmen" of Ephraim (i.e., of the other repository of 'Israel'). Thus, in the "temple sermon," while "all
Judah" is indicted, intimations of their 'Israelite' identity
are omnipresent and, we think, indicative that, for Jeremiah,
it is their embodying 'Israel' that makes them responsible to
the law.

    The "temple sermon" contains an additional feature from
which we infer that Jeremiah holds the covenant people to be
the people of the law. In a study of "The Form and Structure
of the Covenantal Formulations," James Muilenburg has indicated a number of elements characteristic of the covenant
form, among which are: a "stress upon the first and second
persons, the I and the Thou"; "the covenant contingency with
its protasis and apodosis"; and "the use of the infinitive

absolute in the call to hearing."[1] How interesting, then, is

the plea at the beginning of Jeremiah's sermon:

> If you really amend your ways and your deeds, really
> execute justice between men, and neither oppress so-
> journer, orphan, or widow nor shed innocent blood in
> this place, and don't follow other gods to your own
> detriment; then, I will let you dwell in this place,
> in the land which I gave to your fathers . . .
> (7:5-7)

The features fairly leap out at the reader: the conditional

form ("if . . . then"); the infinitive absolute (expressed in

the translation by "really"); the "stress upon the first and

second persons" (underlined for emphasis--a more literal

translation produces even more instances; ". . . if you

really execute justice . . . and sojourner . . . you do not

oppress . . . and innocent blood you do not shed . . ."),

Thus, in a sermon which we have already seen to contain sev-

eral indications that the prophet thinks of those whom he

accuses as 'Israel,' he also addresses an appeal to his

auditors using a covenant form. It is hard to resist the

inference that Jeremiah understands himself to be addressing

the covenant people.

There is a further point. According to Muilenburg, a

persistent feature of the "covenantal Gattung" is "the in-

clusion of apodictic requirements."[2] It is no surprise, then

---

[1]Op. cit., pp. 352-55. Muilenburg's prototype of the
"covenantal Gattung" is Ex. 19:3-6 (p. 352).

[2]Ibid., p. 355.

to find a correspondence in content of Jeremiah's pleas with certain apodictic requirements. He urges the foregoing of apostasy as does apodictic law (Ex. 20:3). The sojourner, orphan, and widow are protected by apodictic law (Ex. 22:20-21; 23:9; Deut. 27:19); Jeremiah pleads with his people no longer to oppress these. Even the shedding of innocent blood may, at one time, have been prohibited by a law in apodictic form.[1] Thus, in 7:5-7, Jeremiah uses a covenant form to appeal to the covenant people to obey the covenant law.

From our study of 2:4-4:2 and 7:1-15, we conclude that, for Jeremiah, the people of the law is the covenant people, 'Israel.' In this, he is like our other prophets; and, like them too, he addresses the entire community (e.g. 7:2), and groups within it (2:8; 6:13; 21:12; 23:14).

But Jeremiah, alone of our prophets, also directs accusations grounded in apodictic law against individuals.[2]

---

[1]The Massoretic form of Deut. 19:10 translates: "that no innocent blood be shed in your land . . ." Gerhard von Rad, in Deuteronomy: A Commentary, tr. by Dorothea Barton (Philadelphia: The Westminster Press, 1966), p. 127, comments: "The whole section ends in v. 10 with a general hortatory warning against all shedding of innocent blood, in which possibly an early apodictic prohibition has been preserved ('Thou shalt not shed innocent blood in your land')."

[2]While the Prophetic Judgment-Speeches of Amos 7:16-17 and Isaiah 22:15-25 are directed against individuals, the accusations are not grounded in apodictic law. Like Jeremiah 20:1-6, these are speeches directed against an opponent of the prophet.

We have already examined the Woe-Speech of 22:13-19
(cp. pp. 62 and 97, above) which is directed to Jehoiakim,
accusing him of behavior which we found to be prohibited by
apodictic law. In so doing, Jeremiah reminds us of the pre-
literary prophets; for they, too, accused kings, and the content of their accusations corresponds to apodictic law (II
Sam. 12:9, murder and adultery; I Kings 11:33, apostasy; 21:
19, murder; II Kings 1:6, apostasy). Even here, however,
there is a difference: the deeds of the kings which precip-
itate the words of judgment of the pre-literary prophets are
all transgressions of the Decalogue, while the content of
Jeremiah's denunciations of Jehoiakim correspond to apodictic
laws which are not found in the Decalogue (see p. 62, above).
These remarks aside, what is of moment to us here is that
Jeremiah does ground an accusation against an <u>individual</u> king
in apodictic law.

In 29:23, Jeremiah declares one reason for his an-
anouncing the death of the prophets Ahab and Zedekiah at the
hand of Nebuchadrezzar to be that ". . . they have committed
adultery with their neighbor's wives." Jeremiah evidently
spent a good deal of his time delivering judgment-speeches
against prophetic opponents (e.g. 20:1-6; 28:12-16; 29:29-32).
The gist of his accusation in these speeches is that his opponents "have prophesied falsely" (cp. 20:6; 28:15; 29:31);
and here, too, we find it as an accusation, along with the

accusation of adultery (29:23; cp. vs. 21).[1] Indeed, we
suspect that Ahab's and Zedekiah's having "prophesied falsely" is to be understood as the real ground for the announcement of judgment, and that the intent of the charge of adultery is to discredit the message by discrediting the messengers. Nevertheless, the charge of adultery is certainly
formally part of the accusation, so that we have this second
instance in Jeremiah of an individual (i.e., two individuals)
being the object of an accusation grounded in apodictic law.

So then, where the content of Jeremiah's accusations
corresponds to apodictic law, the list of the "accused" includes: the whole people, groups, two prophets, and one
king.

Our concern in the present chapter has been to ascertain whom our prophets consider to be bound by the law.
Our answer is that, for them, the people of the law is the
covenant people, 'Israel.' Along the way we have also
learned that, with the exception of two passages in Jeremiah,
it is always the whole community or groups within it whom our
prophets accuse of having violated the law.

---

[1]The word שקר, present in the Massoretic text in 29:
21, 23, is not translated in the LXX. Nevertheless, even omitting שקר from vs. 23, the remaining accusation, "they
spoke a word in my name which I didn't command them," represents a charge of falsifying prophecy, if not of "proph-
esying falsely."

PART II.   THE PROPHETS AND THE LAW

IV. THE PROPHETS AND THE LAW

. . . (when you give alms), do not let your left
hand know what your right hand is doing.
                                    (Matt. 6:3)

The text applies the advice to the domain of charity
but, for us, it has served as a guide to procedure. Let us
explain. Our inquiry has been concerned with what we have
called, "The Law in the Prophets." Basic to this inquiry has
been a search; for the "law" in which we have been interested
does not take the form of law at all. When a student of the
Bible thinks of law he thinks of one of the stipulations of
the Decalogue, or one of the laws in casuistic form. The
prophets, however, talk about things which have not been done
or about things which have been done which should not have
been done. The starting point of our investigation was the
observation that the content of a particular prophet's accusation corresponded closely to certain Pentateuchal laws.
This observation led us to read other accusations and to compare their content with the laws of the Pentateuch.[1] Our
findings are presented in tabular form on the next two pages.
The table indicates: 1) a summary of the content of

---

[1]See chapter I, above.

Accusation	Prophetic Passages	Pentateuchal Legislation
Oppression (of the poor)	Am. 2:7a; 3:9-10; 4:1; 5:11; 8:4 Mic. 2:2 Is. 1:17; 3:15; 10:1 Jer. 6:6; 21:12; 22:3; 23:17	Ex. 22:20-21; 23:9 Lv. 19:13 Dt. 24:14
Interest on loans	Am. 5:11	Ex. 22:24 Lv. 25:36-37 Dt. 23:20
Perversion of justice	Am. 2:7; 5:7, 10, 12; 6:12 Mic. 3:1, 9 Is. 5:23; 10:2 Jer. 5:28	Ex. 23:1-3, 6-7 Lv. 19:15 Dt. 16:19
Unjust weights	Am. 8:5 Mic. 6:10-11	Lv. 19:35-36 Dt. 25:13-15
Disregarding law of pledge	Am. 2:8 Mic. 2:8	Ex. 22:25 Dt. 24:17b
Accepting bribes	Mic. 3:11; 7:3 Is. 1:23; 5:23	Ex. 23:8 Dt. 16:19; 27:25
Disregard of property rights	Mic. 2:2, 9 Is. 5:8	Ex. 20:17 Dt. 27:17
Mistreatment of alien/orphan/ widow	Mic. 2:8-9 Is. 1:17, 23; 10:2 Jer. 5:28; 7:6; 22:3	Ex. 22:20-21; 23:9 Lv. 19:33 Dt. 24:17; 27:19
Disrespect of parents	Mic. 7:6	Ex. 20:12; 21:15; 21:17 Dt. 27:16
Lying	Mic. 6:12 Jer. 6:13; 8:10; 9:4; 23:14	Lv. 19:11c
Sorcery	Mic. 5:11	Ex. 22:17 Dt. 18:10

Accusation	Prophetic Passages	Pentateuchal Legislation
Soothsaying	Mic. 5:11 Is. 2:6	Lv. 19:26 Dt. 18:10
Images	Mic. 1:7; 5:12 Is. 10:10 Jer. 8:19	Ex. 20:4 Lv. 26:1 Dt. 27:15
Pillars	Mic. 5:12	Dt. 16:22 Lv. 26:1
Asherim	Mic. 5:13 Jer. 17:2	Dt. 16:21
Murder	Is. 1:21 Jer. 7:9	Ex. 20:13; 21:12 Dt. 27:24
Idolatry	Is. 2:8, 18, 20 Jer. 1:16	Lv. 19:4; 26:1
Stealing	Is. 1:23 Jer. 7:9	Ex. 20:15 Lv. 19:11a
Shedding inno- cent blood	Jer. 2:34; 7:6; 22:17	Dt. 19:10
Adultery	Jer. 3:8-9; 5:7-8; 7:9; 9:1; 13:27; 23:10, 14; 29:23	Ex. 20:14 Lv. 20:10
Swearing falsely	Jer. 5:2; 7:9	Ex. 20:7; 20:16 Lv. 19:12
Child sacrifice	Jer. 7:31; 19:5; 32:35	Lv. 18:21; 20:2 Dt. 18:10
Talebearing	Jer. 6:28; 9:3	Lv. 19:16
Not paying wages	Jer. 22:13	Lv. 19:13 Dt. 24:14-15
Apostasy	Jer. 2:4-4:2; etc. Cp. Isaiah's indictment of alliances with Egypt	Ex. 20:3

prophetic accusations whose content corresponds to that of
certain Pentateuchal laws; 2) the prophetic passages where
each accusation is found; 3) the corresponding Pentateuchal
legislation.[1] Thus, it is from comparison with the Pentateuchal legislation--used as a control--that we have inferred
"The Law in the Prophets." Now, in order to make this comparison, one needs two hands: using the Hebrew Bible, one
places his left hand upon the prophetic citation and his
right hand upon the comparable Pentateuchal law(s). Having
made the comparison, however, it was almost entirely with the
left hand--our prophetic hand--that our work proceeded and,
with one notable exception, it has been the findings of our
left hand that we have recorded. The exception was the finding of the right hand--our Pentateuchal hand--that where
there is a correspondence in content between prophetic accusation and Pentateuchal legislation, the form of the legislation is always apodictic.

Nevertheless, just as our left hand was wont to examine
the context surrounding the prophetic accusation on which it

---

[1]We have omitted Amos' accusation (2:7b) of father and
son having intercourse with the same girl since, though it is
contrary to the spirit of several apodictic laws, it is not
expressly forbidden by any one law (cp. pp. 106-107, above).
And, while we have included Jeremiah's accusation of
"swearing falsely" (7:9), since we do not know what Jeremiah
is indicting thereby, we are unwilling to fix upon one of the
cited Pentateuchal laws as that to which Jeremiah was referring (see our discussion of השבע לשקר in fn. 1, p. 61,
above) and so have listed the three possibilities.

had focused and to record its findings; so did our right hand
examine the context surrounding the Pentateuchal law(s) on
which it had focused and record its findings. These findings
now claim our attention; first as observations, then for the
light they throw upon the relationship of the prophets to the
law. We are about to let our left hand know what our right
hand has been doing.

Laws in the Law

One of the first things noted by our Pentateuchal hand
was that it kept returning to the same places; i.e., that
these laws in apodictic form whose content corresponded to
certain prophetic accusations were grouped together--they
occur in series.[1] The perusal of these series leads, in turn
to further observations.

The first observation is that these series are created.
Alt makes this point in relation to the מות יומת series of

---

[1]Two types of apodictic series--the comprehensive and
the specialized--have been differentiated by Alt, using content as the criterion ("Die Ursprünge," pp. 319-321; cp. the
second paragraph in our text, below). Of the 59 Pentateuchal
references in the table on pp. 179-180, above, 20 are to the
comprehensive lists (the Decalogue, the scattered מות יומת
series, the Curse Dodecalogue). There are 11 references to
Lev. 19, which contains a potpourri of short specialized
lists (cp. von Rad, Studies in Deuteronomy, pp. 27-30), and 9
to the Covenant Code (exclusive of the מות יומת series),
which likewise contains small collections of apodictic laws
(e.g., Ex. 22:20-21; 22:24-25; 23:1-3, 6-9). Two-thirds of
the Pentateuchal references are located in just six chapters
(Ex. 20-23; Lev. 19; Deut. 27).

Ex. 21:12 ff. and in contrast to casuistic law:

> Dann wird die Distanz vom kasuistischen Recht noch
> wesentlich grosser; denn so gewiss auch diesem die
> Tendenz zur Verknüpfung seiner einzelnen Bestimmung-
> en innewohnt, wie vor allem das Corpus im Bundesbuch
> zeigt, so wenig arbeitet es doch mit derart sinnen-
> fälligen Verknüpfungsmitteln, sondern vertraut al-
> lein auf die zwingende Wirkung seiner juristischen
> Systematik.[1]

The age of particular series and whether in a given instance
we are dealing with an oral or literary creation are matters
of dispute; but, since the Covenant Code contains series in
apodictic form, the creative process is antecedent to it.[2]

Further, the creative process was accompanied by a
process of selection. The inference was drawn by Alt from
a comparison of the content of the Decalogue, the reconstructed מות יומת series, and the Curse Dodecalogue of Deut.
27.[3] Noting that each list was compiled with the intention

---

[1]"Die Ursprünge," p. 311.

[2]For example: Gerhard von Rad (Deuteronomy, p. 167),
calls the Curse Dodecalogue ". . . the most ancient series of
prohibitions preserved for us in the Old Testament"; while,
for Georg Fohrer (Introduction, p. 143; cp. 70), ". . . it
came into being in the Deuteronomic period, and is therefore
far from being the most archaic series of prohibitions in the
OT." For a brief survey of the varied views as to the age
and origin of the Decalogue, see J. J. Stamm, Ten Commandments, pp. 22-35. A ninth century date is generally agreed
upon for the origin of the Covenant Code (cp. Fohrer, Introduction, p. 137); i.e., anterior to Amos.

[3]For the reconstructed מות יומת series and the comparison of its content with that of the Decalogue and Curse
Dodecalogue, see the table prepared by Alt in "Die Ursprünge,"
p. 320.

of being comprehensive, and that each was inhibited from completeness because there was a limit upon the number of clauses which a list could contain, he concludes: "So muss in jedem Fall aus dem zu reichen Stoff eine Auswahl getroffen werden."[1] This lack of completeness was compensated for by special lists of narrower compass. Examples of these more specialized series are: regulations governing the Israelite in the legal assembly (Ex. 23:1-3, 6-9); forbidden sexual relationships (Lev. 18:7-17); harvest regulations (Lev. 19:9-10); demands for justice and charity (Lev. 19:13-18).[2]

If it is correct that the series of laws in apodictic form suggest a process of creation and selection, then they must also involve an element of _decision_. But, upon what grounds was a decision to be made? The special series suggest that germaneness was an important factor; i.e., in a list of harvest regulations, the prohibition of murder would be irrelevant. On the other hand, in a comprehensive series, the criterion of importance would have assumed significance.

There follows from our discussion a corollary: if there was a process of creation, of selection, of decision-making, of distinguishing the germane and important from the

---

[1]Ibid., pp. 319-20. The quotation is from p. 320. Alt thinks that the normal list consisted of twelve clauses.

[2]In Studies in Deuteronomy, pp. 25-36, von Rad gives several examples of such specialized series which he has extracted from the Holiness Code.

187

irrelevant and less important, then <u>there</u> <u>must</u> <u>have</u> <u>been</u> <u>a</u> <u>freedom</u> <u>to</u> <u>do</u> <u>these</u> <u>things</u>.

There is a final observation which is prompted by the occurrence of laws in apodictic form in series: the serialization reflects a purpose. Things are put together in series as an aid to retention; i.e., series reflect a didactic intent.[1] But, there is instruction, and there is instruction; and here, the formal tone of apodictic law makes clear that we are dealing with an instruction whose intent is to inculcate obedience. The hortatory tone is evident in each of the four types of apodictic law: the monotonously repetitive מות יומת; the ringing ארור, emphasized by its position at the beginning of the sentence; and the direct address and emphatic negative of the type exemplified by the series of Lev. 18: 7-17, features which also belong to the Decalogue type.[2]

Let us summarize the reflections stemming from the observation of our right hand that Pentateuchal laws in

---

[1]Cp. Walther Zimmerli, The Law and the Prophets, trans. by R. E. Clements (Oxford: Basil Blackwell, 1965), pp. 36-37: "Why, for example, are there exactly ten commandments? . . . The number ten was arrived at, not for the sake of some high idea, but for the sake of the quite practical necessity of better retention. The Decalogue was . . . a collection of ten injunctions put together for practical catechetical reasons."

[2]For the characteristic features of the four types of apodictic law, see Alt, "Die Ursprünge," pp. 307-19 (cp. our summary on p. 3, above). Alt has grasped the essential quality common to all four: they always express a categorical prohibition (p. 322).

apodictic form occur in series: there was, in Israel, a
process of instruction in the "law," the intent of which was
to inculcate obedience; a process involving selection, and
implying, in turn, a freedom to make such selection--to set
apart that which was deemed to be of special significance.[1]
These reflections our right hand cheerfully bequeaths to our
left and prophetic hand.

Another finding of our Pentateuchal hand may be stated
as follows: though several laws may have the same form, the
Pentateuch does not attach the same significance to each of
them. This finding is based upon an assumption: the importance of a law may be estimated by the consequences prescribed for its breach. To illustrate, let us consider the
following stipulations which bear a close formal resemblance:

You shall not murder (Ex. 20:13).

You shall not boil a kid in its mother's milk.
(Ex. 23:19)

---

[1]The provenance of this instruction and its agents have
been matters of scholarly investigation. For us, it is the
fact and its implications that are important. For the thesis
that this instruction was connected with a prophetic "office,"
see: Hans-Joachim Kraus, Die prophetische Verkündigung des
Rechts in Israel (Zollikon: Evangelischer Verlag AG, 1957);
James Muilenburg, "The 'Office' of the Prophet in Ancient
Israel," in The Bible in Modern Scholarship, ed. by J. Philip
Hyatt (Nashville: Abingdon Press, 1965), pp. 74-97; Murray
Newman, "The Prophetic Call of Samuel," Israel's Prophetic
Heritage, ed. by Bernhard W. Anderson and Walter Harrelson
(New York: Harper & Brothers, 1962), pp. 86-97.

You shall not go about as a talebearer among your
people (Lev. 19:16).

Formally, each makes an equal claim to obedience and one
might assume, from this formal resemblance, that they are of
equal significance; but, the evidence of the Pentateuch is
otherwise. Of the three, only for the first does the Pentateuch record the consequence of its breach:

Whoever strikes a man mortally shall be put to
death (Ex. 21:12).

Mendenhall has pointed out that the Covenant Code shows that
nearly all of the stipulations of the Decalogue are "protected" by such "legal sanctions."[1] Thus, no later than the
time of the Covenant Code, the Decalogue seems to have had a
special significance.

The special place occupied by the Decalogue has been
examined further in a recent study by Anthony Phillips, in
which he argues that "the Decalogue constituted ancient
Israel's pre-exilic criminal law code . . .," the punishment
for the breach of any of its stipulations being death.[2]
During the pre-exilic period, other "crimes" were added for
whose breach the death penalty was to be exacted (e.g., the
prohibition of bestiality; Ex. 22:18), though none "which

---

[1]Law and Covenant, p. 15: "The fact is that nearly all
the stipulations of the Decalogue are here (i.e., in the Covenant Code) protected. Omitted are the false use of the name
of Yahweh and the prohibition of coveting."

[2]Criminal Law, p. 1.

could not be derived from the Decalogue."[1]

A similar _effective_ distinction may be inferred from the Curse Dodecalogue of Deut. 27:15-26. These things are not just things which, like other things, should not be done; but are deemed to be of such significance that--though they may be perpetrated in secret and thus not subject to punishment by the community--God is asked to deal with the offender.[2]

Thus, the Pentateuch affords evidence that some laws were thought of as having a special significance in that, for their breach, punishment is prescribed or envisioned. An observation of Yehezkel Kaufmann is pertinent in this context.

Kaufmann argues that biblical books can be grouped into units on the basis of "idea-constants" which appear in them and distinguish them from books of other groupings.[3] In

---

[1]_Ibid._ Phillips contends that the intent of bestiality (originally a practice associated with Canaanite ritual) was to effect physical union with Yahweh. Its prohibition is therefore to be understood as an extension of those commandments (the commandments forbidding a פסל and the improper use of Yahweh's name) whose purpose was to maintain Yahweh's freedom from the control of man (p. 121).

[2]Having observed that the prohibitions of the Curse Dodecalogue also appear ". . . elsewhere in the early Israelite legal traditions," Gerhard von Rad concludes ". . . that we have here a collection of precepts which were significant in forming a pattern for the common life of those who worshipped Yahweh" (_Deuteronomy_, p. 168). But, such a _collection_, implies a _selection_--a separating of the more, from the less important. For the relationship between "secret" crimes and divine punishment, see pp. 197-198, below.

[3]_Religion of Israel_, p. 157.

particular, he distinguishes what he calls the "Torah-group"
(the Pentateuch and the Former Prophets) from the prophetic
literature.[1] One of the differences which Kaufmann sees has
to do with the types of sin which are deemed to have historical consequences on a national scale. He says:

> . . . in the books of the Torah-group, the moral
> principle does not reach the level of a historically
> decisive factor. The writers do not draw conse-
> quences for national history from their moral prin-
> ciples. For the Torah-group the moral factor is not
> . . . equal in historical importance to the relig-
> ious-cultic.[2]

Kaufmann proceeds to set forth those "sins" which the Torah
declares to be "clauses of national punishment and exile":
"the cultic defection of the golden calf"; "the lack of faith
in YHWH shown in the episode of the spies"; the "sins of
'impurity'" of Lev. 18 and 20; and, in Deuteronomy, "the sin
of idolatry" (we would prefer the more comprehensive term,
"apostasy"), "the crucial national sin."[3] While, in Lev. 26,
"'all the statutes and judgments' are spoken of," and "the
warning of Deuteronomy 28 includes 'all the commands and the
statutes,'" the explicit mention of the others suggests, to
Kaufmann, the priority given to them by the Torah.[4]

---

[1]Ibid.

[2]Ibid., p. 160.

[3]Ibid., p. 159. The passages which Kaufmann cites from
Deuteronomy (where exile is threatened for idolatry) are: 4:
25 ff.; 6:10 ff.; 7:1 ff.; 8:19 ff.; 11:16 ff.; 28:14, 20,
47, 58 (p. 159).

[4]Ibid.

If, as Kaufmann has observed, the Torah seems to place
a special emphasis upon idolatry/apostasy and the "sins of
'impurity,'" one is led to wonder if this is to be attributed
to an intrinsic quality which makes these "sins" more heinous
than, for example, disregarding the sabbath or murder. Of
such there is no indication. However, the passages which
warn against these offenses and state the consequences of
disobedience do have in common two interesting features.

First, they impute the behavior against which they warn
to the pre-Israelite inhabitants of the land and/or those who
will be Israel's neighbors when she occupies the land. So
the parenetic section, Lev. 18:24-30, with respect to the
"abominations" which are prohibited by the legislation contained in vss. 6-23: "The inhabitants of the land who preceded you committed all these abominations" (18:27). So too
with the warning against other gods. These are not just
other gods, but the gods of Israel's neighbors (Deut. 6:14)
and predecessors in the land (Deut. 7:1-5). Now while it is
difficult to establish a causal nexus between the fact that
these offenses are characteristic of Israel's predecessors/
neighbors and the fact of their being deemed to hold national
consequences for Israel should she be foolish enough to
commit them, the texts do seem to reveal an operative prin-
ciple in the divine economy which is of universal application;
i.e., if Israel does what the "nations" have done (do), she

193

will experience what they have experienced (will experience):

> Do not defile yourselves by any of these things
> . . . (for the inhabitants of the land who preced-
> ed you committed all these abominations and defiled
> the land), lest the land vomit you forth when you
> defile it, as it vomited forth the nation which pre-
> ceded you (Lev. 18:24, 27-28).

> Should you forget the Lord your God to follow other
> gods, serving and worshiping them, I give you solemn
> warning this very day, that you shall utterly perish--
> just like the nations whom the Lord is about to cause
> to perish before you.
> (Deut. 8:19-20)

Thus, to Kaufmann's view that these "sins" are characterized
as bearing special consequences for Israel should she commit
them, we would add the observation that they are distinguished, also, as being components of the culture of Israel's
land.

The second feature is this: when one reads the incident of the "golden calf," the parenetic material of Lev. 18:
24-30, or Kaufmann's examples from the Torah which connect
the sin of apostasy with the consequence of national disaster,
one becomes aware not only that the consequences of the "sin"
effect the total community, but of the involvement of the
total community (stated or anticipated) in the "sin." In the
"golden calf" incident, only Moses was not involved. Lev. 18:
29 states the consequences to accrue to any individual who
transgresses any of the prohibitions of vss. 6-23: "Anyone
who commits any of these abominations--such persons shall be

194

cut off prematurely from their people."[1] The verses surrounding it (24-28, 30), however, have a different focus:
they tell what happens to <u>nations</u> which commit such abominations (vs. 24; cp. vs. 27), and that Israel, too, if she is
similarly culpable, should expect identical consequences (see
above, pp. 190-191). That is, the passage envisages two
situations--when an individual "sins" and when a people "sin"
--and states the consequences of each.

The situation is similar in Deuteronomy with respect to
apostasy. 17:2-7 stipulates what is to be done to an individual offender, while 13:12-17a prescribes the punishment for
an apostate city. In both cases it is the guilty, alone,
upon whom punishment is to fall. In contrast, 7:1-4 is concerned with the possible contamination of the <u>whole people</u>
with apostasy as a result of intermarriage with the pre-
Israelite inhabitants of the land. Should such a thing come
to pass, the destruction of the entire people would be its
consequence (7:4b). Like the latter passage in connecting
national disaster with <u>national</u> apostasy is Deut. 29:21-27.[2]
At issue is the cause of the national catastrophe which has

---

[1]Matitiahu Tsevat has shown that the meaning of biblical <u>kareth</u> is "premature death," in "Studies in the Book of
Samuel, I," <u>HUCA</u>, XXXII (1961), pp. 191-214, <u>passim</u>.

[2]For the form and provenance of this pericope, see
Burke O. Long, "Two Question and Answer Schemata in the
Prophets," <u>JBL</u>, XC (June, 1971), pp. 130-31.

made the land a desolation (vss. 21-23). Pourquoi?

> (Because) . . . they have gone and served other
> gods and worshiped them, gods whom they have not
> known--who were not allotted to them (29:25).

It was because <u>they</u> had committed apostasy that the <u>whole</u> land
was despoiled: <u>since the sin had permeated the entire community, destruction had overtaken the entire community</u>.
Thus, we would hold that, in dealing with those passages
which attribute historical consequences on a national scale
to certain sins, one must give weight not only to what was
done (Kaufmann), but to "who done it."

A brief attempt at recapitulation is in order. Our
discussion (pp. 186-193) has evolved from the assumption that
the importance of a law may be estimated by the consequences
prescribed for its breach. By this criterion, the Decalogue
seems to hold a special place; for, elsewhere in the Pentateuch, many of its stipulations are upheld by the death penalty. In a similar way, the Curse Dodecalogue raises certain
stipulations to prominence. The observation of Kaufmann that
in the Torah (-group), the "sins of 'impurity'" and "the sin
of idolatry" are deemed to evoke consequences on a national
scale, needs some qualification. Especially is it noticeable
that, in the Torah, the very passages which attribute national
consequences to these "sins" conceive of them as having been
committed by, or running rampant within, the entire nation.
Thus, while these "sins" and, ipso facto, the legislation

which prohibits them are (based on our assumption) accorded a
primacy by virtue of their consequential nature, the fact of
national involvement in these sins must be given weight as
contributing to their eminence. Finally (and here we move
on), in contemplating, or recounting, disobedience on a
national scale, the passages which have come under recent
scrutiny differ markedly from the Pentateuchal legislation
itself. To this further observation of our Pentateuchal hand
we must now turn.

The Pentateuchal legislation in apodictic form is addressed to individuals and, insofar as it stipulates or in-
vokes punishment, it is always the disobedience of the individual that is contemplated. The latter point may be il-
lustrated by an example from the מות יומת series and one from
the Curse Dodecalogue. In each, the singular is used of the
agent of the offense:

> Whoever strikes a man mortally shall be put to
> death (Ex. 21:12).

> Cursed be he who slays his neighbor secretly.
> (Deut. 27:24)

With respect to the former point, however, the prohibitions
confront us with two difficulties. The first may be introduced by way of Martin Noth's comment at the beginning of his
discussion of Ex. 20:3:

> The prohibition of "other gods" is the basic de-
> mand made of Israel, who is addressed here, as in

197

what follows, in the collective second person.[1]

Who is the "thou" who is addressed in the Decalogue? Is it,
as Noth would have it, "Israel"? And, if so, are we then
wrong in insisting that apodictic law is addressed to individuals? Now, of course, the answer is that we are dealing not
with an either/or, but with a both/and. Assuming a covenant
context for the Decalogue, the "thou" is Israel; but, at the
same time, logic demands that it is the individual to whom
the warning is pertinent. The logic is set forth in
Gerstenberger's discussion of the "singular prohibitives":

> Eine Prüfung der singularischen Prohibitive selbst
> macht es sehr wahrscheinlich, dass sie auf den
> einzelnen hin gesprochen sind. . . . Denn: . . .
> Die verbotenen Handlungen sind wesentlich solche,
> die von einem einzelnen und ohne Mithilfe anderer
> ausgeführt werden können, die so in den Verantwort-
> ungsbereich des Individuums fallen. Eine kollek-
> tive, korporative Deutung von Taten, wie sie durch
> die Verben חמד (Ex. 20:17); נאף (Ex. 20:14); לחץ,
> ינה (Ex. 22:20; Lev. 19:33); קלל (Ex. 22:27; Lev.
> 19:14) usw. beschrieben sind, würde sich durch den
> Aussagegehalt dieser Verben selbst ad absurdum
> Führen.[2]

The second problem the prohibitions pose for the thesis that
apodictic law in the Pentateuch is addressed to individuals
is what is to be made of the fact that they occur in the
plural as well as the singular.[3] Again, the solution is

---

[1]Exodus, p. 162.

[2]Wesen und Herkunft, pp. 66-67.

[3]For prohibitions in plural form, cp. Lev. 19:11-12,
26-28.

offered by Gerstenberger:

> Die Prohibitive in der 2.P. Plural ... sind
> grösstenteils auf das Konto von späteren Schreib-
> ern, die sich eines paränetischen Stils bedienen,
> zu setzen.[1]

That is, the difference is stylistic, not substantive.

We conclude, therefore, that it is with the behavior of
the individual that apodictic law in the Pentateuch is concerned.

The following passage provides a point of embarkation
for the final observation of our Pentateuchal hand:

> Any Israelite, or sojourner in Israel, who of-
> fers any of his progeny to Molech shall be put
> to death; the people of the land shall stone
> him. I myself will turn against that man and
> cut him off prematurely from among his people,
> because he has offered one of his progeny to
> Molech . . . (Lev. 20:2-3).

Here, in consecutive verses, the punishment of the transgressor of an apodictic law is declared to be the business
of different agents; and, what is here presented in nuce, is
characteristic of the Pentateuch as a whole: sometimes the
community is the punitive agent, at other times, God. However, before we become concerned by the apparent superfluity
of executioners or the possibility of double jeopardy, let us
examine the situations in which God or people appear (or are
called upon) to exact punishment.

It is clear immediately, that, in the normal situation,

---

[1] Wesen und Herkunft, p. 67.

the punitive agent is the community. For example, Deut. 17:
2-7 and 21:18-21 record the procedures for the conviction and
punishment of an apostate, and of a rebellious son, respectively. In each case, the punishment of death is carried out
by the community (17:7; 21:21). The case of Naboth, in which
we see the law in action, accords with this (I Kings 21:13b).

The passages to which we have just referred illustrate
the way in which justice was supposed to be, or actually was,
carried out in Israel--apprehension, conviction, and punishment of the criminal by the community.[1] Unfortunately, justice is another realm in which there's opportunity for "many
a slip 'twixt the cup and the lip"--with the result that one
who breaks the law may not drink the hemlock. Such situations we may call, in contrast to the above, abnormal situations. For these situations in which the result of a transgression is not (or would not be) the punishment of the offender by the community, various Pentateuchal passages invoke
articulate, or describe an alternative mode of justice--the
punishment of the offender is reserved to God.

Abnormal Situation 1. What is to happen when the community
is unaware that a transgression has been committed?

We cited earlier (p. 194) two pieces of apodictic

------

[1]It would be difficult to convince Naboth that justice
was operative in his case; nevertheless, correct procedure
was followed.

legislation which deal with the subject of murder:

Whoever strikes a man mortally shall be put to
death. (Ex. 21:12)

Cursed be he who slays his neighbor secretly.
(Deut. 27:24)

Though the passages are alike in the subject with which they
deal and in the intention that the murderer be punished, they
differ in respect to the agent by which the punishment is to
be effected. The assumption of the first passage is that
punishment will be effected by the community. The verse from
Deuteronomy, however, reserves the punishment to God who is
the agent by which the curse is made effective.[1] What accounts for the difference is the word "secretly," as Alt
points out in commenting upon the Curse Dodecalogue:

Und bemerkenswert ist . . ., dass es sich hier
durchweg um Verbrechen handelt, die im Geheimen
begangen werden und daher Aussicht haben, niemals
vor eine menschliche Gerichtsbarkeit zu kommen.
Daher hat es seinen guten Grund, dass die Sätze
hier nicht wie in der anderen Reihe (the מות יומת
series) auf eine von der Volksgemeinschaft zu
vollstreckende Todestrafe hinauslaufen, sondern
auf die Verfluchung des Täters, . . . Das Ent-
scheidende zur Verwirklichung dieser Flüche hat
demnach im gegebenen Falle Jahwe zu tun, zu des-
sen Kenntnis ja auch die im Verborgenen geschaeh-
enden Untaten kommen . . .[2]

Abnormal Situation 2. What is to happen when the community

---

[1]For the view that, despite the passive construction,
God executes the curse, see Herbert C. Brichto, _The Problem
of "Curse" in the Hebrew Bible_ (Philadelphia: Society of
Biblical Literature, 1963), pp. 211-15.

[2]"Die Ursprünge," p. 314.

does not carry out its responsibility to punish the transgressor? It is this abnormal situation that lies behind the
announcement of Yahweh in the passage from Leviticus with
which we began our discussion (p. 196, above), as the verses
which follow it in the text are quick to point out:[1]

> If the people of the land should hide their eyes
> from that man--even ever so slightly--when he of-
> fers one of his progény to Molech, so as not to
> (have to) put him to death; I myself will turn
> against that man and his kin, and will cut off
> prematurely from among their people both him and
> all who follow him in whoring after Molech
> (Lev. 20:4-5).

If the community abdicates its responsibility, God will see
that justice is done!

Abnormal Situation 3. What is to happen to someone who does
something that is prohibited but, because no punishment is
prescribed, incurs no liability? One might, for example, be
inclined to disregard the prohibitions of Ex. 22:20-21 which
protect the alien, widow, and orphan from exploitation. He
who would do so, however, must still reckon with God:

> If you do mistreat him, as soon as he cries out
> to me I'll hear, and become outraged, and put you
> to the sword; and your wives will become widows,
> and your children orphans (Ex. 22:22-23).

Abnormal Situation 4. What is to happen when the normal

---

[1]In Leviticus: A Commentary, trans. by J. E. Anderson
(London: SCM Press, 1965), pp. 148-49, Martin Noth points
out that 20:2b-5 is ". . . obviously not a unity." Vss. 4-5
resolve the tension between vs. 2 which states that the community is to put the offender to death, and vs. 3, where God
announces that he will exact punishment.

punitive agent is, itself, culpable?--i.e., what is to happen
when the community (or a substantial portion of it) is guilty
of breaking the law? We noted above (pp. 191-193) that one
of the features of those passages which attribute national
consequences to the sin of apostasy is that they also conceive of the involvement of the total community in the sin.
Who is it, according to these passages, who exacts punishment?

> Then the Lord sent a plague upon the people, be-
> cause they had made the calf . . .[1] (Ex. 32:35).

> Be careful not to be enticed into serving and
> worshiping other gods. For the Lord would be-
> come outraged at you, and would restrain the
> skies so that there would be no rain and the
> ground would not yield its produce, and you
> would perish quickly from the land . . .[2]
> (Deut. 11:16-17)

In society, when the offender is the one normally responsible
for punishing those who commit the offense he has committed,
there is a problem. Our texts from Ex. 32 and Deuteronomy
tell us that, in just such a situation,--the offense being
apostasy and the offender Israel--God becomes the executioner.

To summarize: According to normal legal procedure as
assumed and revealed by the Pentateuch, when an offender is

---

[1]The verse continues: ". . . which Aaron had made."
We have omitted these words as secondary. Cp. Noth, Exodus,
p. 244.

[2]Other passages in Deuteronomy which state that God
will punish the community for its apostasy are: 6:14-15;
7:4; 8:19-20; 29:24-27.

convicted for an offense for which the punishment is death,
the community is the agent for exacting punishment. There
are, however, what may be called abnormal situations when,
though an apodictic law has been broken, circumstances may
allow the offender to go free. In these abnormal situations,
the Pentateuch reveals a tendency to reserve punishment to
God.

This we now add to the other observations of our Pentateuchal hand and, armed with the findings of our earlier
chapters as well, return to our prophets.[1]

The Prophets and the Law

When Amos appears at Temple Bethel and announces the
imminent destruction of the northern kingdom, the words he
uses to explain the reason for this catastrophe bear a strong
resemblance in content to some of the apodictic legislation
of the Covenant Code. When Jeremiah appears at Temple Jerusalem, announcing its imminent destruction, the words he uses
to explain the reason for this catastrophe bear a strong
resemblance to some of the prohibitions of that piece of
apodictic legislation which we call the Decalogue. Though
Amos and Jeremiah are separated by more than a century and
represent the beginning and end of our prophetic spectrum,
and though the laws which their words recall are found in

---

[1]"Our prophets" are Amos, Micah, Isaiah, and Jeremiah.

different pieces of Pentateuchal legislation, in their
speaking they, and Micah and Isaiah as well, hold certain
features in common.

The first of these features which our prophets hold in
common is that they are alike in what precedes their speaking
Here we must include: the presupposition of their speaking;
the occasion for their speaking; and the impetus to their
speaking.

The speaking of our prophets presupposes that their
auditors are conversant with those apodictic laws (or an
earlier form of them) whose content is similar to that of
the prophet's accusation(s). The view that Amos' accusations
presuppose certain prohibitions of the Covenant Code and
Jeremiah's Temple Sermon the Decalogue meets with no chronological impediments, for the bulk of the Covenant Code antedates Amos' ministry, and the Decalogue that of Jeremiah.[1]
When one comes, for example, to Amos' indictment of unjust
weights (8:5b) vis-à-vis the apodictic prohibitions of Lev.
19:35-36 (Holiness Code) and Deut. 25:13-15, the question of
chronological priority becomes more difficult. Nevertheless,
once one accepts the canon that even the latest legal corpora
may contain early material, then one must reckon seriously
with the possibility that either or both laws antedate the

---

[1]That the Covenant Code antedates Amos is generally
accepted. See fn. 2. p. 183. above.

Amos passage.[1] Indeed, one might argue: since the laws of
the Covenant Code whose content is similar to Amos' accusations do antedate these accusations, then, unless one can
definitely establish the chronological posteriority of these
laws whose content is similar to an accusation of Amos, it is
probable that they, too, precede; particularly if the exigen-
cies of logic require their priority. And, according to R.
E. Clements, such is the case:

> The accusations which Amos raised against the peo-
> ple . . . would have carried no weight whatever if
> these demands for righteousness and justice were
> not already familiar to them.[2]

Since Amos is the earliest of our prophets, and the Holiness
Code is usually considered to be the latest of those codes

---

[1]The legal corpora (Covenant Code, Deuteronomic Code,
Holiness Code, Priestly Code) represent the end results of
lengthy processes of compilation. Behind these stand smaller
collections of, for the most part, individual laws. Thus,
for example, when Eissfeldt discusses the date of origin of
the Holiness Code, he says: "(The individual) . . . commands
are all, or at any rate for the most part, old or even very
old, . . ." (Introduction, p. 237). For the formation of
the larger and smaller units and the problem of dating the
collections and the individual laws, see the Introductions of
Bentzen, Eissfeldt, and Fohrer.

[2]Prophecy and Covenant, p. 76. Eichrodt ("Prophet and
Covenant," p. 187) maintains that Isaiah's message likewise
presupposes the people's knowledge of God's commands: "Knowledge of the divine commandments is here taken for granted
and does not need to be mentioned. This is the common ground
of faith which allows the prophet to conduct his argument
from agreed premisses."

which contain laws similar in content to the accusations of
our prophets, we consider the argument set forth above sufficient to sustain our proposition. It may be summarized as
follows: The chronological priority of the Covenant Code to
Amos and the Decalogue to Jeremiah show that some laws in
apodictic form antedate prophetic accusations whose content
is similar to them. Since they _are_ prior, the prophet's
accusations _can_ presuppose them. Logic demands that they _do_
presuppose them.

Behind the speaking of our prophets lies the dissemination of apodictic law to the people. How this was done
does not concern us; only _that_ it was done.[1] What occasions
their speaking may be explained by recalling the distinction
made earlier in this chapter between what we called the normal and the abnormal situation (pp. 196-197); the abnormal
situation being one in which a transgression of apodictic law
did not result in the punishment of the transgressor by the
community. It is precisely such an abnormal situation that
evokes the prophetic message:

> There must always have been individuals who broke
> the commandments; these the law dealt with. Now,
> however, at one fell swoop not individuals but the
> whole of Israel--or at least her leading men--were

---

[1]For the view that the proclamation of apodictic law
was a function of a prophetic office, see fn. 1, p. 186,
above.

sharply accused of flagrant breaches of the law.[1]
Our discussion in the previous chapter has confirmed. this
observation of von Rad: it is almost always the total community, or groups within it, whom our prophets accuse.[2] The
time of our prophets is not a normal time. When the enforcer
is the transgressor, transgression does not result in punishment.[3] It is this situation which occasions our prophets'
speaking.

But, our prophets were men. There were other men to
whom the situation which occasioned our prophets' speaking
was visible, but they did not speak. Our prophets tell us
that there was an impetus to their speaking--that they were
impelled to speak:

> The Lord took me . . . and said, "Begin prophesy-
> ing to my people Israel" (Amos 7:15).
>
> But as for me, I am filled with power . . .
> To declare to Jacob his rebellion,
> To Israel his sin (Micah 3:8).
>
> I heard the Lord say, "Whom shall I send . . ."
> So I said, "You win. Send me" (Isaiah 6:9).
>
> You compelled me to sit alone,

---

[1]Gerhard von Rad, Old Testament Theology, II, p. 136.

[2]See above, pp. 149-176, passim.

[3]The situation is similar when the king is the transgressor, as is the divine solution: God sends a prophet to
announce judgment (cp. pp. 13-14, above).

For you filled me with rage (Jeremiah 15:17).[1]
What happens in the world can be seen by every man. Our
prophets stood out from other men in that they spoke about
what they saw. And the reason they gave for their speaking
was--God.

When we listen to our prophets speak, it is much like
arriving in the middle of a play: there are certain significant things that have gone on before which provide the
setting for what we see. We have attempted to isolate the
things that precede our prophets' speaking. The people whom
they address, though knowing what the law requires, have
broken it. Yet, inasmuch as the people are themselves responsible for upholding the law, they go unpunished. Our
prophets see and, driven by divine impulsion, speak.

The second feature which our prophets hold in common
is that they are alike in what happens in their speaking.
The previous sentence is a carefully worded attempt to steer
our course between Scylla and Charybdis: between the necessity of engaging in a detailed study of the question of the
prophetic office (is his essential function that of e.g.,
"messenger," "covenant-mediator," "vizier," etc.) and/or of
the "Sitz im Leben" of the PJS (cult, court, international

---

[1]I.e., ". . . er ist ganz erfüllt von göttlichem Zorn
(=6:11) und schaut deshalb nichts als Unheil und Gericht"
(Rudolph, Jeremia, p. 92).

law, etc.).[1] That is, we are concerned not with the uniform
a prophet wears when he speaks, nor with tracing the lineage
of the formal vehicle of his speaking, but solely with what
that speaking accomplishes. We see as happening in the
speaking of our prophets two things and a third. We begin
with the second of the two things.

Our prophets announce that certain disasters, whose
author and/or agent is God, will befall their people (or
groups, or king).[2] Jeremiah 7:20 is one such announcement,
other examples of which may be found scattered throughout
our first two chapters:

> Therefore, thus says the Lord God: Take notice
> that my tempestuous wrath is about to be poured
> out upon this place, encompassing man and beast
> . . .

---

[1]Literature dealing with the question of the prophetic
office includes: Klaus Baltzer, "Considerations Regarding
the Office and Calling of the Prophet," HTR, 61 (1968), pp.
567-81; Julien Harvey, Le Plaidoyer prophétique, pp. 145-53;
John S. Holladay, Jr., "Assyrian Statecraft and the Prophets
of Israel," HTR, 63 (1970), pp. 29-51; James Muilenburg, "The
'Office' of the Prophet in Ancient Israel"; Rolf Rendtorff,
"Botenformel und Botenspruch"; James Ross, "The Prophet as
Yahweh's Messenger," Israel's Prophetic Heritage, pp. 98-107;
Claus Westermann, Grundformen, pp. 70-91. Relevant to the
issue of the "Sitz im Leben" of the PJS are: Harvey, Le
Plaidoyer prophétique (international law); Westermann,
Grundformen (court); Ernst Würthwein, "Der Ursprung der
prophetischen Gerichtsrede" (cult). We have summarized
Westermann's view, along with his criticism of Würthwein, on
pp. 11-13, above.

[2]For God as the author/agent of the disasters announced
by the prophets, see above, pp. 79-88.

Now, while it is interesting to observe that a number of
features which are characteristic of a message (MF; the p
ence of חנה /"take notice"; use of the first person) aɪ
present in these words of Jeremiah, and from this to conɪ
that this was understood as a message, and then to consi....
whether the prophet was a messenger or was simply delivering
a message in the performance of some other role; and while it
might be of interest to discuss whether what is being conveyec
by these words is threat or decision;[1] nevertheless, the
point is that what happens in these words is that the auditors are apprised that they are on the verge of experiencing
a calamity whose source is God.

Is this disaster which is to be effected by God for-
tuitous? The first thing that happens in the speaking of our
prophets is the establishment of the <u>cause</u> of which the impending disaster is the <u>consequence</u>:

> The children gather wood while the fathers kindle
> the fire and the women knead dough, to prepare
> cakes for the queen of heaven; and they pour out
> libations to other gods, with the result that I
> am provoked (Jer. 7:18).

We have followed Westermann in referring to this first
part of the PJS as the Accusation. However, it must be recognized that it is more than this. It is also less. It is
less, in that it is, at first sight, merely a recounting of

---

[1]For these matters, see the literature cited in fn. 1,
p. 207, above.

behavior. It is more, in that--since the behavior which is recounted is contrary to apodictic law--like the testimony of the witness for the prosecution in a trial (cp. I Kings 21:13), the recounting establishes the fact of transgression.[1]

To summarize: The first thing that happens in Jeremiah's speech (which we have chosen as an example of our prophets' speaking) is that he recounts the behavior of the people; behavior which is contrary to apodictic law. The second thing that happens is that he announces as the consequence of this (cp. "therefore"; 7:20) the people's imminent destruction by God. Thus, our prophets establish a causal relationship between what the people (or groups, or king) have done and what God is about to do.

But, of course, one might wonder on what grounds it is proper that what our prophets announce that God is about to do should be the consequence of what they say the people have done. If our prophets had done nothing more than establish a causal relationship, they would have been mere providers of information. But, they went on to take the further step of justifying the disasters they announce. And, that is the third thing that happens in the speaking of our prophets.

The process by which the disasters are justified in-

---

[1]Cp. the following statements of Westermann in Grundformen: 1) "(eine Anklage) . . . besteht in der blossen Feststellung eines Tatbestandes" (p. 94); 2) "die Anklage ein . . ., gerade geschehenes Vergehen nennt" (p. 95).

volves two reminders. First, our prophets remind these
people whom they say that God is about to destroy that they
are 'Israel'; a people for whom God had done special things,
and to whom he is related by covenant (cp. Amos 2:9-10; Mic.
6:4; Is. 1:2; Jer. 2:6-7. For our consideration of the evidence on which this statement is based, see chapter 3, above).
Second, they remind them that the things they have done, of
which the disasters are the consequence, amount to a breach
of the covenant relationship: These things they have done
constitute פשע (see above, pp. 104-116) and לא ידע (pp.
116-123); these things can properly constitute the basis for
instituting a Covenant Lawsuit (pp. 123-145); the consequences of these things are to be disasters whose contents
parallel treaty-curses (pp. 93-104). By the language they
use and the images they evoke, our prophets set the behavior
of their people and its consequence in the context of the
covenant, so that what they announce as about to happen is
not just the consequence of what has been done; but, because
their people are who they are and have done what they have
done, its just consequence--the action of a covenant sovereign against his recalcitrant vassal.

Our prophets speak in an abnormal situation and announce an abnormal way of God's dealing with his people. The
normal way was the way of "Heilsgeschichte"; now, it is to be
"Unheilsgeschichte." 'Israel' has no one but herself to

213

blame. What God is about to do is justified, for his people have transgressed the law and broken the covenant thereby.

The final feature held in common by our prophets is that they are alike in what their speaking implies.

In discussing apodictic law in its Pentateuchal setting, we noticed that, while laws having the same form make the same claim to obedience, the Pentateuch elsewhere attributed a greater significance to some than to others. The criterion for this was the consequences prescribed for a law's breach (cp. pp. 186-187, above). With this criterion in mind, it is noticeable that, in no case, does the accusation portion of any of the Prophetic Judgment-Speeches of our prophets correspond in content to any of the cultic requirements of apodictic law. None of our prophets says, "Because you have boiled a kid in its mother's milk, therefore . . ."; or, "You have not kept the feast of unleavened bread, therefore . . ." How are we to account for this lack of reference in our prophets to the breach of the cultic requirements of apodictic law, and what does it mean?

One possibility, of course, is that the people didn't disobey the cultic requirements of apodictic law. Indeed, there is plenty of evidence from our prophets that the people took their ritual seriously. Since the prophets did inveigh against syncretistic elements in the cult, and did speak out when the cult was used as a surrogate for obedience to the

moral requirements of apodictic law, their silence with respect to the cultic requirements of apodictic law can only
mean that these were obeyed.[1]

Another possible way of accounting for the lack of
prophetic reference to the breach of the cultic requirements
of apodictic law is to see it as a reflection of the prophets' own belief: for them, cultic requirements were the mere
accoutrements of religion, not religion itself. For the
prophets, the cult was an impediment to true religion; therefore, its requirements were no longer valid.[2]

While either of the above might account for the phenomenon we have observed, we think that the real reason lies
elsewhere, for what we are about to suggest explains not only
this phenomenon, but something else as well. We mentioned
earlier Alt's comparison of the content of the Decalogue, the
reconstructed מות יומת series, and the Curse Dodecalogue,
and his conclusion that the intent of each was to be comprehensive (pp. 183-184, above). When one reads these comprehensive lists of apodictic legislation, one finds all sorts
of concern with apostasy/idolatry and with morality/ethics,

---

[1]For the prophetic indictment of the cult when used as
a surrogate for obedience to the moral requirements of apodictic law, see pp. 129-130 and 143-144, above.

[2]For the prophetic view of the cult characterized in
this paragraph, see the works cited by Clements (Prophecy and
Covenant, p. 95, fn. 1) and Harvey (Le Plaidoyer prophétique,
p. 97, fn. 4).

215

but not a single law dealing with cultic regulations. Martin Noth, focusing on the Decalogue's omission of these regulations, has this to say:

> The lack of special cultic requirements is noteworthy. This corresponds to the fact that in the Old Testament cultic action is indeed generally presupposed as a possible, even a requisite way of worship, but that the special and unique element in the relationship between God and Israel is not evident in the cultic sphere but in the obedience to the one God and his demands which pertain to human relationships. Even the sabbath commandment is no exception here, for whatever may have been the significance of the sabbath in the view of the Decalogue it was at all events not thought of as a cultic feast.[1]

If Noth is correct, then there is a tradition which does not understand cultic requirements to be an essential part of the relationship between God and Israel; a tradition to which both the absence of cultic regulations in the comprehensive lists and the silence of our prophets regarding the breach of the cultic requirements of apodictic law attest. Just as the Pentateuch imputes to some apodictic laws more significance than others (see above, pp. 186-189), so also do our prophets (or rather, in this case, less); for by them, cultic requirements are relegated to second place--or even to no place.

Are the prophets progenitors of a tradition which understands obedience to cultic requirements to be nonessential to

---

[1]*Exodus*, p. 167.

the relationship between God and Israel, or are they its progeny? Two of our prophets state clearly that they are heir:

> Was it sacrifices and offerings you brought me those forty years in the wilderness, O house of Israel (Amos 5:25)?

> I neither spoke to your fathers nor charged them concerning matters of burnt offering and sacrifice when I brought them out of the land of Egypt (Jer. 7:22).

Thus, the speaking of our prophets (and their non-speaking) implies that God does not care about the requirements of cult.

Quite different is our prophets' view of the ethical requirements of apodictic law. Certain observations drawn from our invasion of the Pentateuch when set beside what we find to be the case in our prophets illumine the prophetic view.

In the Pentateuch, even though laws having a formal similarity make the same claim to obedience, the consequences ascribed by the Pentateuch to their breach set apart some as being more significant than others. If one were to ask the Pentateuch which of the following ethical requirements was the more consequential,

> You shall not murder (Ex. 20:13).

> You shall not go about as a talebearer among your people (Lev. 19:16).

it would point to the first; for while the Pentateuch nowhere

217

records that the talebearer is to be punished, it stipulates that the murderer is to be put to death (Ex. 21:12).

For Jeremiah, however, both are consequential; he indicts his people for both (murder in 7:9 and talebearing in 9:3), and each is a contributing factor to a disaster which the prophet announces (7:14; 9:6 ff.). And, Jeremiah's attitude toward talebearing is matched by that of Amos and Micah with regard to the prohibition of unjust weights, and by all four of our prophets with reference to the laws which prohibit perversion of justice.[1] That is, ethical requirements of apodictic law which are regarded by the Pentateuch as _inconsequential_ have become _consequential_ in our prophets.

Further, whereas in the Pentateuch only the sin of apostasy is said to have historical consequences on a national scale, in our prophets, transgression of the ethical requirements of apodictic law are said to be similarly consequential.[2] Again and again our prophets announce the most

---

[1]The verses which contain the prophetic accusations of the use of unjust weights and the perversion of justice are listed, along with the corresponding Pentateuchal legislation in the table on p. 179, above. While none of the laws there cited stipulates punishment for transgression, the prophets announce punishment for those whom they accuse.

[2]The Pentateuchal view has been detailed in our discussion of Kaufmann's observation on pp. 188-189, above. Sample passages from our prophets where national disaster is announced as the consequence of transgression of the ethical requirements of apodictic law are: Amos 2:6-8, 13-16; Micah 6:9-16; Isaiah 1:21-25; Jer. 7:8-15.

horrible national disasters as the consequence of behavior
contrary to these requirements. This statement must, of
course, be qualified in the same way as was the Pentateuchal
observation: just as those Pentateuchal passages which declare national disaster to be the consequence of apostasy
perceive the sin of apostasy as infecting the entire community, so our prophets see ethical transgression as having
infected their people.[1]

Finally, while according to the Pentateuch breach of
the ethical requirements of apodictic law may engender, as
the case may be, no punishment, death inflicted by the community, or, in abnormal situations, punishment by God; our
prophets state that, for behavior contrary to the ethical
requirements of apodictic law (whether punishment is stipulated in the Pentateuch or not), God will inflict punishment.[2]

---

[1]Our qualification of the Pentateuchal observation is
chronicled on pp. 191-193, above. In the prophetic passages
cited in the previous footnote (where national disaster is
announced as the consequence of transgression of the ethical
requirements of apodictic law), the community is, in each
case (cp. Amos 2:6; Micah 6:9; Isaiah 1:21; Jer. 7:2), the
accused. To be sure, e.g., in Micah 3:9-12 national disaster
is announced as the consequence of the leaders' transgressions. However, as was pointed out above (pp. 160-161),
Micah ultimately comes to see that all are guilty.

[2]Cp., again, the prophetic passages listed in fn. 2,
p. 215, above. In each (Amos 2:13; Micah 6:13-14; Isaiah 1:
24-25; Jer. 7:14-15), it is said that God will, himself,
effect punishment. Notice, too, that what was the exception
in the Pentateuch (punishment was reserved to God in abnormal
situations; cp. pp. 197-200, above) has become the rule in
the prophets. This is because, in the prophets, the abnormal

Thus, in a variety of ways, our prophets' speaking attributes the greatest significance to the ethical requirements of apodictic law. They agree that, while God may not care about cult, he is a stickler when it comes to ethics.

The statement of the final implication of our prophets' speaking must be prefaced by an observation. The placing of a law on the books or its dissemination by proclamation is only an expression of intent. This is true no matter if it be a law of man or of God. However, when someone says, "Because you have done this, such and such will happen to you," they remove the law that prohibits such behavior from the realm of the hypothetical and place it in the realm of the practical. Thus, when our prophets announce that God is about to exact punishment for behavior contrary to certain laws (apodictic laws which prohibit apostasy and its forms of expression, and various ethical requirements of apodictic law), they move beyond an understanding which sees them as the will of God for his people to imply that God really does care about these laws. And, of course, this has its corollary: since God cares, his people should too.

---

situation (the guilty escaping punishment) has become the prevailing one.

220

V.   CONCLUDING SUMMARY

With the end of the consideration of our prophets'
speaking, our speaking is at an end as well. We must now
bring together what we have said.

1. When one reads the prophetic words of judgment, one is
surprised that there is no complaint about the propriety of
the indictment. That is, the people apparently did these
things, and were wrong in so doing. But, this implies that
there was a standard to which the people were committed and
by which they might be judged.

2. A look at the content of the Accusation portion (which
stipulates what the "accused" has done wrong) of the Prophetic Judgment-Speeches of Amos, Micah, Isaiah, and Jeremiah
reveals a correspondence in content to certain Pentateuchal
laws. In every case, the Pentateuchal form of these laws is
either apodictic or, in a few instances, an original apodictic form may be seen to underlie the present form. This suggests that apodictic law may have formed the standard we have
surmised.

3. What is so special about these laws? They are part of
the covenant between God and 'Israel.' Our prophets establish the covenant-connection in three ways. First, by the

221

language they use. The behavior for which they indict their people--behavior which is contrary to apodictic law--constitutes פשע and "not knowing" (לא ידע) God, and the language of a number of the disasters announced as consequences of this behavior is paralleled in treaty-curses. Second, by the use of a form. Micah, Isaiah, and Jeremiah each institute a Covenant Lawsuit indicting their people for behavior contrary to apodictic law. Third, by establishing what it is about the accused that makes him indictable. The accused is, or is a part of, 'Israel,' the covenant community. If behavior by the covenant people or its representatives which is contrary to apodictic law is grounds for a Covenant Lawsuit; amounts to "rebellion" against, and not recognizing the authority of, a covenant sovereign; and, results in the activation of covenant-curses; then, that law must be part of the covenant.

4. Were one to look only at those Pentateuchal laws in apodictic form that do correspond in content to our prophets' accusations, one might be led to an incorrect inference: i.e., that apodictic law and covenant law are co-extensive. However, a look at the Pentateuch reveals a number of apodictic laws dealing with cultic requirements, none of which is paralleled in content in the accusations of our prophets. When this is set beside the observation that the comprehensive series of Pentateuchal apodictic legislation lack any cultic requirements, one explanation is able to account for

222

both phenomena: there was a tradition for which the ritual
requirements of apodictic law were not part of the covenant.
From this we must conclude that, while the content of prophetic accusation does correspond to that of certain apodictic
laws, covenant tradition formed the real basis of our prophets' accusations.[1] The correspondence in content may be
explained on the assumption that that tradition included the
proclamation of laws whose form was apodictic.

5. If, on the one hand, our prophets are heirs of a tradition that obedience to the demands of cult are not decisive
for the relationship between God and 'Israel'; on the other,
they yoke the ethical requirements of apodictic law firmly to
that relationship: not just those which are singled out as
the more important by their place on the comprehensive lists
and/or by the death penalty imposed for their disobedience;
but those of the complementary lists and those that stipulate
no punishment as well. Our prophets see disobedience to
these ethical requirements as having national consequences,
for they see this disobedience as having infected the nation.

6. By placing the behavior of their people in the context

---

[1]Casuistic law, also, was not originally part of the
covenant tradition; therefore, as we have seen, the content
of prophetic accusation does not correspond to any casuistic
laws. As far as our prophets were concerned, the transgression of a casuistic law--like the transgression of a
ritual requirement of apodictic law--would have had no effect
upon the covenant relationship.

of the covenant, our prophets established their people's
guilt, explained the disasters they announced, and justified
the God who was their author. In so doing, they proclaimed
in a new way the demands of God for his people, so that, insofar as disaster was not God's final word--their acceptance
of the covenant obligations still being possible--there was
opened for 'Israel' the way to life.

SELECTED BIBLIOGRAPHY

Books

Alt, Albrecht. _Kleine Schriften zur Geschichte des Volkes Israels_, I. München: C. H. Beck'sche Verlagsbuchhandlung, 1953.

Anderson, Bernhard W. and Harrelson, Walter, ed. _Israel's Prophetic Heritage: Essays in Honor of James Muilenburg_. New York: Harper & Brothers, 1962.

Bentzen, Aage. _Introduction to the Old Testament_. 2 vols. 5th ed. Copenhagen: G. E. C. Gad, 1959.

Bewer, Julius A. _The Prophets_. (Harper's Annotated Bible Series.) New York: Harper & Brothers, 1955.

Beyerlin, Walter. _Die Kulttraditionen Israels in der Verkündigung des Propheten Micha_. Göttingen: Vandenhoeck & Ruprecht, 1959.

Blank, Sheldon H. _Jeremiah: Man and Prophet_. Cincinnati: Hebrew Union College Press, 1961.

Bright, John. _Jeremiah_. (The Anchor Bible, Vol. 21.) Garden City, New York: Doubleday & Company, Inc., 1965.

Buttenwieser, Moses. _The Prophets of Israel_. New York: The MacMillan Company, 1914.

Clements, R. E. _Prophecy and Covenant_. (Studies in Biblical Theology, 1st Series, No. 43.) London: SCM Press, Ltd., 1965.

Eissfeldt, Otto. _The Old Testament: An Introduction_. Translated by Peter R. Ackroyd. New York: Harper & Row, Publishers, 1965.

Fohrer, Georg. _Introduction to the Old Testament_. Translated by David E. Green. Nashville: Abingdon Press, 1968.

Gerstenberger, Erhard. _Wesen und Herkunft des sogennanten apodiktischen Rechts im Alten Testament_. Bonn: Rheinische Friedrich-Wilhelms Universität, 1961.

226

Gray, George Buchanan. A Critical and Exegetical Commentary on the Book of Isaiah, I-XXXIX: Vol. I, Introduction, and Commentary on I-XXVII. (The International Critical Commentary.) New York:
Charles Scribner's Sons, 1912.

Harper, William Rainey. A Critical and Exegetical Commentary on Amos and Hosea. (The International Critical
Commentary.) New York: Charles Scribner's Sons, 1910.

Harvey, Julien. Le Plaidoyer prophétique contre Israël
après la rupture de l'alliance. (Studia: Travaux
de recherche, Vol. 22.) Bruges: Desclée de
Brouwer and Montréal: Les Éditions Bellarmin, 1967.

Hillers, Delbert R. Covenant: The History of a Biblical
Idea. Baltimore: The Johns Hopkins Press, 1969.

_____. Treaty-Curses and the Old Testament Prophets.
(Biblica et Orientalia, N. 16.) Rome: Pontifical
Biblical Institute, 1964.

Kaufmann, Yehezkel. The Religion of Israel. Translated
and abridged by Moshe Greenberg. Chicago: The
University of Chicago Press, 1960.

Kissane, Edward J. The Book of Isaiah, Vol. I. Dublin:
The Richview Press for Browne and Nolan Limited, 1960.

Koch, Klaus. The Growth of the Biblical Tradition. Translated by S. M. Cupitt. New York: Charles Scribner's
Sons, 1969.

Kraus, Hans-Joachim. Die prophetische Verkündigung des
Rechts in Israel. (Theologische Studien, Heft
51.) Zollikon: Evangelischer Verlag AG, 1957.

Lindblom, Johannes. Prophecy in Ancient Israel. Oxford:
Basil Blackwell, 1962.

Maag, Victor. Text, Wortschatz und Begriffswelt des
Buches Amos. Leiden: E. J. Brill, 1951.

McCarthy, Dennis J. Treaty and Covenant. (Analecta
Biblica, 21.) Rome: Pontifical Biblical Institute, 1963.

Mays, James Luther. Amos: A Commentary. (The Old Testament Library.) Philadelphia: The Westminster
Press, 1969.

Mendenhall, George E. _Law and Covenant in Israel and the Ancient Near East_. Pittsburgh: The Biblical Colloquium, 1955.

Nielsen, Eduard. _Oral Tradition_. (Studies in Biblical Theology, 1st Series, No. 11.) London: SCM Press, Ltd., 1961.

_____. _The Ten Commandments in New Perspective_. Translated by David J. Bourke. (Studies in Biblical Theology, 2nd Series, No. 7.) Naperville, Ill.: Alec R. Allenson, Inc., 1968.

Peake, A. S. _Jeremiah and Lamentations_. 2 vols. (The New Century Bible.) New York: Henry Frowde, 1910.

Phillips, Anthony. _Ancient Israel's Criminal Law_. Oxford: Basil Blackwell, 1970.

Noth, Martin. _Exodus: A Commentary_. Translated by J. S. Bowden. (The Old Testament Library.) London: SCM Press, Ltd., 1962.

_____. _The Laws in the Pentateuch and Other Studies_. Translated by D. R. Ap-Thomas. Edinburgh and London: Oliver & Boyd, 1966.

_____. _Leviticus: A Commentary_. Translated by J. E. Anderson. London: SCM Press, Ltd., 1965.

Rad, Gerhard von. _Deuteronomy: A Commentary_. Translated by Dorothea Barton. (The Old Testament Library.) Philadelphia: The Westminster Press, 1966.

_____. _The Problem of the Hexateuch and Other Essays_. Translated by E. W. Trueman Dicken. Edinburgh and London: Oliver & Boyd, 1965.

_____. _Studies in Deuteronomy_. Translated by David Stalker. (Studies in Biblical Theology, 1st Series, No. 9.) London: SCM Press, Ltd., 1956.

Rudolph, Wilhelm. _Jeremia_. (Handbuch zum Alten Testament, Erste Reihe, 12) Tübingen: J. C. B. Mohr (Paul Siebeck), 1947.

Smith, John Merlin Powis; Ward, William Hayes; and Bewer,
    Julius A. A Critical and Exegetical Commentary on
    Micah, Zephaniah, Nahum, Habakkuk, Obadiah and Joel.
    (The International Critical Commentary.) New York:
    Charles Scribner's Sons, 1911.

Snaith, Norman H. The Distinctive Ideas of the Old Testa-
    ment. New York: Schocken Books, 1964.

Stamm, J. J. The Ten Commandments in Recent Research.
    Translated with additions by M. E. Andrew.
    (Studies in Biblical Theology, 2nd Series, No. 2.)
    London: SCM Press, Ltd., 1967.

Volz, Paul. Der Prophet Jeremia. (Kommentar zum Alten
    Testament.) Leipzig: A. Deichertsche Verlags-
    buchhandlung, 1928.

Weiser, Artur. The Old Testament: Its Formation and De-
    velopment. Translated by Dorothea Barton. New York:
    Association Press, 1961.

Westermann, Claus. Grundformen prophetischer Rede.
    München: Chr. Kaiser Verlag, 1960.

Zimmerli, Walther. The Law and the Prophets. Translated
    by R. E. Clements. Oxford: Basil Blackwell, 1965.

Articles

Anderson, George W. "Israel: Amphictyony: ʿAM; KAHAL;
    ʿEDAH." Translating & Understanding the Old Testa-
    ment. Edited by Harry Thomas Frank and William L.
    Reed. Nashville: Abingdon Press, 1970, pp. 135-51.

Bach, Robert. "Gottesrecht und weltliches Recht in der
    Verkündigung des Propheten Amos." Festschrift für
    Günther Dehn. Neukirchen: 1957, pp. 23-34.

Cogan, Morton. "A Technical Term for Exposure." JNES, 27
    (April, 1968), pp. 133-35.

Eichrodt, Walther. "Prophet and Covenant: Observations on
    the Exegesis of Isaiah." Proclamation and Presence:
    Old Testament Essays in Honour of Gwynne Henton Davies.
    Edited by John I. Durham and J. R. Porter. Richmond:
    John Knox Press, 1970, pp. 167-88.

Fishbane, Michael. "The Treaty Background of Amos 1:11 and
    Related Matters." JBL, LXXXIX (September, 1970),
    pp. 313-18.

Gerstenberger, Erhard. "Covenant and Commandment." JBL,
    LXXXIV (March, 1965), pp. 38-51.

Gevirtz, Stanley. "West-Semitic Curses and the Problem of
    the Origins of Hebrew Law." VT, XI (April, 1961),
    pp. 137-58.

Hammershaimb, E. "On the Ethics of the Old Testament Pro-
    phets." Supplements to Vetus Testamentum, VII.
    Leiden: E. J. Brill, 1960, pp. 75-101.

Huffmon, Herbert B. "The Covenant Lawsuit in the Prophets."
    JBL, LXXVIII (December, 1959), pp. 285-95.

_____. "The Treaty Background of the Hebrew Yada."
    BASOR, 181 (February, 1966), pp. 31-37.

_____, and Parker, Simon B. "A Further Note on the
    Treaty Background of Hebrew Yada." BASOR, 184
    (December, 1966), pp. 36-38.

Lewy, Julius. "The Biblical Institution of Deror in the
    Light of Akkadian Documents." Eretz-Israel, V.
    Jerusalem: The Israel Exploration Society and
    The Hebrew University, 1958, pp. 21-31.

Limburg, James. "The Root ריב and the Prophetic Lawsuit
    Speeches." JBL, LXXXVIII (September, 1969), pp.
    291-304.

McCarthy, Dennis J. "Notes on the Love of God in Deuter-
    onomy and the Father-Son Relationship between Yahweh
    and Israel." CBQ, XXVII (April, 1965), pp. 144-47.

Mendenhall, George E. "Covenant." IDB, I, pp. 714-23.

Muilenburg, James. "The Form and Structure of the Cov-
    enantal Formulations." VT, IX (October, 1959),
    pp. 347-65.

Paul, Shalom M. "Exod. 21:10 a Threefold Maintenance
    Clause." JNES, 28 (January 1969), pp. 48-53.

Rendtorff, Rolf. "Botenformel und Botenspruch." ZAW
    (1962), pp. 165-77.

Tsevat, Matitiahu. "Studies in the Book of Samuel, I."
    HUCA, XXXII (1961), pp. 191-216.

Williams, Prescott H. "The Fatal and Foolish Exchange:
    Living Water for 'Nothings.'" Austin Seminary
    Bulletin, LXXXI (September, 1965), pp. 3-59.

Woude, A. S. van der. "Micah in Dispute with the Pseudo-
    Prophets." VT, XIX (April, 1969), pp. 244-60.

Würthwein, Ernst. "Amos-Studien." ZAW, 62 (1950), pp.
    10-52.

_____. "Der Ursprung der prophetischen Gerichtsrede."
    ZThK, 49 (1952), pp. 1-15.

WITHDRAWN

CATHOLIC THEOLOGICAL UNION
BS1198.B451974   C002
THE PROPHETS AND THE LAW CINCINNATI

3 0311 00018 2811

WITHDRAWN